T0106205

Fun
with
Stuff

Fun
with
Stuff

BRUCE A. SMITH

iUniverse, Inc.
New York   Bloomington

Fun with Stuff

iUniverse books may be ordered through booksellers or by contacting:
iUniverse
1663 Liberty Drive
Bloomington, IN 47403
www.iuniverse.com
1-800-Authors (1-800-288-4677)

ISBN: 978-1-4401-9644-7 (pbk)
ISBN: 978-1-4401-9645-4 (ebk)

Library of Congress Control Number 2009913246

Printed in the United States of America
iUniverse rev. date: 12/11/09

Also by Bruce A. Smith

The Path of Reason

For Sharron

Without her, this book would never have been possible.

Acknowledgments

Thanks to Kathleen Brackney for spending a considerable amount of time proofreading an early manuscript of mine titled *Fun with Yourself*, parts of which evolved into the *Fun with Stuff* column. Thanks, as well, to the editors (past and present) of *The I.E*, the Inland Empire Mensa bulletin, in which most of these columns were previously printed. These editors, who supported me throughout the first ten years of the column, include Lynda Kay, Sonja Struthers, and Tom Pigeon. Allison St. Clare of Seniorwire.net earns special recognition because it is through her syndication service that several columns were published throughout the United States, as well as in Mumbai, India. Dianna Narciso and Diane Drucker came to my aid at the last minute and provided additional pairs of eyes when mine had become blind to my own mistakes. Also, to the many fans who let me know that you laughed, thank you for your continued encouragement; it has kept the column alive.

Contents

The Wreckreational Vehicle

We had great ambitions when my father-in-law gave us his used RV. We could drive to the Grand Canyon, we thought, or Europe! Europe would be great—maybe Paris. There's nothing like Paris in an RV. But then those who love us advised that a shorter trip might be in order. We decided that a trip to the Pechanga RV Park near Temecula, just ninety miles from our home in Southern California, might be the perfect way to work out the bugs.

We loaded up the RV, started the engine, and turned on the air conditioner. The air conditioner wasn't working. We turned it off and on several times with the same result. We tried it without the engine running. Then we toyed with the generator, flicked various switches, and had little discussions about what could be wrong. We speculated, devised theorems, and checked the oil. None of these seemed to make the air conditioner work.

My wife and I are working on becoming one of those lovable old couples who talk about everything far more than it needs to be talked about, making sure that each point is repeated at least twice. We do this because we enjoy it. If anyone were traveling with us, I am sure we would drive them mad. The broken air conditioner gave us a great opportunity for such discussion. We broke with tradition, however, and actually came to a conclusion, which was to forget the dang air conditioner and drive with the windows open.

We made it safely to Temecula, where we found a man at a convenience store who was more than happy to break the valve on our propane tank, causing ten dollars of propane to whistle and steam its way out into the afternoon sun. My wife commented that it would have been far more fun, if not more profitable, to have put our money into a slot machine.

The man who had "filled" our tank informed us that we had a problem. We asked him if he knew what we could do to *fix* the problem or if he could give us directions to an RV repair shop, but his answers did not seem to correlate with the questions we asked. He did not speak English very well, which comes in real handy when you break someone's propane tank.

We sat on the steps of the convenience store for a half-hour while the tank continued to leak, and the air conditioner continued to not work. I thought of lighting a cigarette, but then I reconsidered because I didn't want the RV to blow up and because I don't smoke. Once the propane tank was empty, we decided that we could cook using the barbecue instead of the stove and that we could take cold showers instead of warm. We would still get by.

The RV Park was only ten minutes down the road. We pulled in, and I began hooking up the connections, only to notice that there were wires dangling from underneath the RV—long, important-looking, electrical wires. They were frayed because they had been dragged down the freeway.

I crawled under the RV, and I noticed something else unusual. Jutting from underneath, just below the toilet, shower, and sink, there were pipes—pipes with no ends on them—pipes that looked suspiciously incomplete.

"Uh, honey," I called, in the understated tone that I tend to use in times of crisis, "I think we have a problem."

I described my findings to my wife. We performed experiments in which she flushed the toilet and ran water down pipes while I watched water splash onto the concrete.

My wife came out of the RV, looked at all the water, and did that thing where you laugh and cry simultaneously.

Turns out we had no disposal tank. It was gone. We knew it was there before when my wife had cleaned out the RV and used the sinks. We doubted that the tank could have fallen off in transit. You'd think we would have noticed something like that or seen the cars in our rearview mirror as they careened off the side of the road trying to avoid being hit by a big black wastewater tank.

The only other option we could think of was that someone had stolen the tank. But why? To me, that seemed comparable to stealing a kitty litter box, and that requires a somewhat demented thief. Months after the incident, we discovered that drug dealers often steal these tanks and use them when making speed. That was one explanation, but it remains uncertain. I expect that, someday, the disappearance of our wastewater tank will be featured on *Unsolved Mysteries*.

We did solve one mystery however. The severed wires explained the broken air conditioner. They also explained the broken refrigerator, which was the source of our next crisis in which we had to run to the store to get a cooler and some ice before all the meat went bad.

Also, it was too windy to barbecue.

We ate out that evening. Dinner conversation revolved around what might have happened had we not discovered that the wastewater tank was missing.

We decided, later that night, that what we had was a metal tent. Without a functional toilet, shower, sink, stove, air conditioner, or refrigerator, that's basically what the RV was. It did have beds though. Thank goodness for that because otherwise the ants wouldn't have had a place to sleep. Maybe that's what they meant by working the bugs out.

My wife described our situation to the man at the office of the RV park, and he agreed that maybe we should leave because we were an embarrassment to the

RV community. He didn't say that last part, but I know he thought it. We did stay the one night; we had to at least do that, but the next morning, we were on the road home. We felt we had already had enough adventure for one trip.

Did I mention that our gas gauge was broken? It was. We ran out of gas on the freeway, on a bridge over the Santa Ana River, in rush hour traffic. It took two tow trucks to get us off the freeway. We were only a mile from our exit.

So that was our trip. We're going to try again next week. Wanna go?

What it Takes to Order a Wedding Dress

1) Go to a minimum of twenty stores and look at dresses. Deal with rude clerks who tell you that no matter how far in the future your wedding is, you should have started shopping earlier. "You'll never get a dress by the year 3000," they'll tell you. "You should have started planning years ago." (Interesting fact: If you are female and your father is an obnoxious car salesman, you are 20 percent more likely to become an obnoxious bridal shop attendant.)

2) Find the perfect dress.

3) Find out that it is too small for you and cannot be re-sized.

4) Repeat step 1.

5) Find the perfect dress.

6) Find out that someone bought it an hour ago, and it is no longer available. The clerk just forgot to take the dress off the rack.

7) Consider having someone make a dress for you.

8) Look at patterns.

9) Find a pattern you like.

10) Shop for and purchase the material for the dress, as well as the sleeves, slip, train, and gauzy parts.

11) Get in a fight over artistic issues with the lady who was going to sew your dress and decide you'd rather buy a dress instead.

12) Repeat step 1.

13) Find the perfect dress that, of course, will need some alterations.

14) Schedule a fitting that allows you enough time to find the shoes and the strapless bra that you will wear with the dress.

15) Look for a strapless bra.

16) Find the perfect bra in a catalog.

17) Call the catalog store and find out that the bra is no longer being made.

18) Give up and go shopping for shoes.

19) Get in a fight with the groom over whether you should wear open-toe or closed-toe shoes.

20) Trip and sprain your ankle while trying on a high-heel pair of shoes.

21) Find shoes you like. Have them and your ankle brace dyed so that they will match the exact color of your wedding dress.

22) Find a bra on Bras.com.

23) Order the bra.

24) Receive the bra in the mail the same day that a friend gives you a bra, which is exactly the same as the one you ordered.

25) Shop for a veil.

26) Fly to Arabia and purchase a veil there because they are the veil experts.

27) Ride a camel back to the plane.

28) Have your dress fitted.

29) Go to psychological counseling because the fitting took place in a glass booth in the middle of the mall.

30) Have the dress cleaned.

31) Spill wine on the dress.

32) Have the dress cleaned.

33) Rent a safe to have the dress stored in.

34) Find a purse to match the dress.

35) The day before the wedding, transfer the contents of your regular purse into the wedding purse. Lose your license in the process.

36) Go to the DMV for a new license. Discover that DMV clerks aren't so bad after all, now that you've spent all that time dealing with dress shop clerks.

37) Put your new license in the wedding purse.

Tada! You are done.

What it Takes to Order a Tuxedo

Walk into the store and say, "I'd like a tux."

That's it.

The Phone Company

Having lived in many places, I have had many phones and many problems with them. Fortunately, my phone service has always been provided by Condescending Buttheads Incorporated (CBI), a division of We Don't Really Care International.

Perhaps you're already sensing some bitterness. Let me provide some examples of service provided by CBI to give you insight into my attitude.

One month, and this is not comic exaggeration, I received a $600 phone bill for calls of a deviant nature to various 900 numbers. As much as I would have liked to have made these calls, I did not, in fact, make them because my wife is around a lot.

Convincing the phone company that I am not a pervert turned out to be a difficult task. They were barely able to mask their cynicism and disdain when asking such questions as, "Is there anybody else in your household who could have made the calls, you filthmonger?"

We were living in an apartment complex at the time, and I found out that both my next door neighbor and my upstairs neighbor had calls to the same number appear on their phone bills. I also discovered that the phone utility room had been broken into. In addition, the calls on my bill overlapped. One call would start at 11:00 PM and end at 11:15 PM, while another would start at 11:05 PM and end at 11:20 PM. Two possibilities occurred to me: either I lived in an apartment complex full of degenerates, and I could travel through time (which I have done before, but not in this instance) *or* somebody had broken into the utility room and done some tricky wiring. This second option seemed the most probable as the police arrested a guy for doing just that.

I tried to convince the phone company of this, but they said, and these were their exact words: "Mr. Smith, that doesn't seem very likely." I literally spent several hours on the phone trying to clear this up, which was a huge waste of time because the people at the phone company do not talk dirty.

The phone company refused to help me, so I did what I do whenever I find myself in trouble; I asked my wife to save my sorry butt. She did, and within several minutes she had convinced the phone company that the charges were incorrect and should be removed. We even ended up with a credit. When I asked my wife why the phone company assumed I was a deviant but believed her, she said, "Because you're a man."

Recently, though, we had another problem in which we were unable to receive collect calls. Just as in the previous situation, we could back up our position with facts. I explained this to my good friends at CBI, but they said, "We're not interested in facts, sir. We only care about wasting your time, asking belittling questions, and making you feel inferior. It's our job." (I may be paraphrasing.)

Again I called upon my wife, but apparently the phone company had adopted a new non-sexist policy of abusing everyone. My wife was fuming when she got off the phone with them. And she was mad too. The phone company had told her, as they told me, that it was not possible to call collect from certain phones, especially jail phones. Thusly, they figured, everyone who was trying to call us collect was calling from jail. We denied this based on the reasoning that it wasn't true.

"Are you sure the people who are calling you aren't calling from jail?" they asked when we denied it.

We were certain. Our growing defensiveness, however, convinced the phone company representatives that they were right. We wouldn't be so defensive if we were telling the truth, now would we? We were obviously in constant contact with many penitentiaries throughout the Southern California area.

The problem still hasn't been resolved, but that's okay because I've moved up in the social world from being a pervert to being a jail bondsman, and what really matters is that I feel better about myself. I only have the good people at the phone company to thank for that. Thank *you*, CBI.

The House

When I was about to purchase my first house, people casually mentioned that owning a house would be "a lot of work" just like they sometimes mention that, after having a child, a couple "may not get a lot of sleep." I believe these to be understatements.

Here is what they should say: "Your house will consume your entire life, and you will never have fun again. I'm warning you! Think about it first!"

And "If you have a baby, you will be so sleep deprived that, not only will you get bags under your eyes, you will get air bags under your eyes. You will need these because you will undoubtedly fall asleep while driving!"

But no, people are far too subtle about these things.

Owning a house is a lot of work. For us, it would be much easier if the previous occupants had taken care of certain things. "The previous occupants" is a phrase I now use with distaste. If I am outside, I spit after I say it. I avoid spitting inside the house, although it probably wouldn't make much difference. I am quite certain, from the condition of our carpet, that the previous owners ran a petting zoo solely for animals with intestinal problems.

I envision a Yak who lived up to his name and a bear named Poo. I'm also sure there was a goat.

Technically, the house is still a petting zoo of sorts; the animals are just smaller. We got rid of the termites so that the ants would have a place to live. I like to think that it is the "ant elite" who get to come into the house, while the lower class ants hang out in the yard doing manual labor like moving the leaves from the neighbor's tree into our yard.

Snails have a reputation for being slow, but I suspect that they speed things up in private, judging by the rate at which they reproduce. They are getting out of hand at our place. We have one that is the size of a collie. I call him "Bucky," and I go out to pet him now and then. We also have a lot of mushrooms in our yard, so Bucky may or may not be real. I'm not sure.

The pigeons remain a constant problem. We put up one of those plastic owls so they have something to snuggle with. Sometimes the neighbor's cat comes over and has tea and bran muffins with them. Again, the mushrooms may be a factor here.

Speaking of the yard, I also think that the previous occupants (Achh…patoo!) intentionally planted fifteen different varieties of grass as some sort of weird botanical experiment. This was either before or after they sabotaged the sprinklers, broke the oven, and poured honey on the blinds.

That's not to say we don't love our house. We love it. We really do. But just because you love your child doesn't mean you have to like its poopy diapers. I read that somewhere.

So. Let's close with this final image: Before the house was sold to us, I suspect that it was serviced by the Laurel and Hardy Painting Company. I can see Laurel tripping on the bathroom rug and spilling paint all over the shower wall, or Hardy getting hit in the head with a ladder, spilling paint on the bricks in front of the fireplace. As Laurel slides down the banister, there is, no doubt, a huge splotch of paint on his backside that causes audience members to laugh uproariously. The film ends with the two buddies chasing each other down the walkway, paint splashing on the concrete and into the flower beds. As they pass beyond the gate, a circular closing screen narrows down to focus on Laurel's behind, where the paint splotch now forms the words "The End."

At least, that's how I picture it.

The Carpet

One of the things my wife and I did not like about our house when we bought it was the carpet. Sharron said it looked like a paper bag, as if someone had decided to cover the concrete with sacks leftover from a trip to the grocery store. I speculated that after they had carefully taped the paper sacks to the foundation, they let animals run over it, perhaps in a reenactment of a wildlife stampede on the African savannah. I was certain that in our hallway there was the footprint of a rhinoceros.

The first time we ordered new carpet, we discovered it was so expensive that, if we actually bought it, we would not have enough money left over to eat. We would starve to death, and eventually the police would find us dead in our living room.

"They don't look so good," one of them would say.

"Yeah," his partner would answer, "but just look at that carpet!"

The second time we ordered carpet, the carpet company sent Dumbo the elephant to measure the house for us. That may sound harsh at first, but it is so unerringly accurate that I have difficulty feeling any remorse. The first thing he said upon entering our house was, "Why am I here?"

Those were his exact words.

Sharron gave him a befuddled look. She didn't say anything, in hopes that he would elaborate.

I had heard him from the other room, and I walked in to stare at him. *What do you mean, "Why are you here?"* I wanted to ask. *Do you mean that in a cosmic sense?*

He stood there and looked around. A thought popped into his mind. "The people at the office didn't tell me what I was doing here," he said.

"You're measuring the carpet," Sharron explained.

"Where?"

A thousand smart aleck answers raced through my mind, down into my throat, and banged themselves silly against the inside of my mouth as they tried to get out:

We want you to measure the people's house next door. We're buying them carpet as a surprise!

The back yard. We're tired of mowing and thought carpet would be a good look.

In the two bathtubs and under the fish tank. Nowhere else, though. That would be silly.

Sharron spoke up. "See this paper sack on the floor."

"Uh," said the carpet guy.

"We'd like that replaced with a carpet."

That was simple enough for him, and he began measuring. He was fine for a little while, but there was still an air of non-professionalism about him. Perhaps he was an imposter, I thought—some guy who pretends to measure houses for fun, or who was casing our home for a robbery. Suspicious, I followed him up the stairs.

Our loft was a problem for him. To get to it you have to climb up the rungs of a wooden ladder. He asked if I could go up and measure for him.

"Sure," I said. From the loft, I gave the measurements in inches.

"Can you give those to me in feet and inches?" he asked.

The smart-aleck answers busily got themselves into another traffic jam: *Would you like me to write them down for you and call them in to your company? Then I can drive you around in your truck and do the rest of your job for you too!* I smiled and gave him the measurements he wanted.

On his way out, Dumbo the non-flying elephant told us all the things we'd have to do in preparation for the carpet replacement. He was surprised that we considered them to be inconvenient. We knew it would be a lot of work, but by the time he was through, I had the feeling that it might just be easier to move to another house that had nicer carpet.

Two seconds after he walked out the door, Sharron let fly, and that's how the carpet company lost our business.

It was months later when we had the emotional strength to go through the process of, again, picking out carpet and having the house measured. When we did, we were pleasantly surprised.

The guy who was performing the measurements showed up at the door and said, "Hi, my name is George, and I'm here to measure your carpet today. Where exactly would you like me to measure? Are you replacing the existing carpet? Here is a list of things that need to be done before the carpet can be installed. I realize it's a lot of work, but we think you will be happy with the results. You can review that while I begin taking my measurements. Do you mind if I go upstairs? I see on my notes here that you have a loft and would like that measured separately. I'll go up and check it out. Thank you. Have a nice day."

"Now that's what I'm talking about," I said to my wife. She nodded, and we shared a secret smile.

Everything would have been perfect except for one item the carpet guy mentioned in passing. "If you are planning on doing any painting," he said, "you'll want to give yourselves time to do it before the installation date."

Painting! I thought. That part had not even occurred to me. Sharron had thought of it but had avoided mentioning it for fear of sending me over the edge.

Luckily, the house was in good shape, except for the wooden railing that runs along the stairway and the edge of the loft. There were splatters of white paint all over the wood. There were also great big white blotches on the railing where it met the walls, a healthy warning that you should never drink and paint.

While cleaning the paint off the rails in the loft, Sharron noticed that there was something more than just white paint on some of the wood. "This is bird poo!" she exclaimed. And right she was. The family who owned the house before us must have had a pet bird as well. My earlier image of an African stampede suddenly became more detailed. Now it included chimpanzees wielding paintbrushes and flocks of birds circling under the high ceiling. Dumbo would have felt right at home.

Once cleaned, the railing was ready to be re-stained. Upon opening the can of wood stain, I noticed the word "Pleistocene" but didn't think anything of it. I figured it was one of the ingredients in lacquer. Two days later, when the wood stain still wasn't dry, I read it again. The can said, "If you do not know what you are doing and you apply this stain in thick coats to wood that was previously stained, the length of time it will take for this stain to dry is equivalent to the length of the geologic era known as the 'Pleistocene.'"

That was a long time, and that was a problem. The carpet people were due to install the carpet in a day, and the stain would not be dry by then. There was no way they could lay the carpet when the ladder to the loft, as well as all the railings in the house, were covered with wet wood stain. The stain had already ruined two sets of clothes, including my dress with the fancy flower print and the matching shoes.

We had to reschedule the installation. Fortunately, when the day for it finally arrived, it went off without a hitch. I appreciated this because it allowed me to resume my new exercise program called "moving things in and out of the garage and up and down the stairs." It's a great program. There are no monthly dues and no annoying personal trainers who talk down to you even though you could kick their butts in a spelling bee. So, now that our house is fit for company, maybe, someday, I will be too.

A Curious Phrase

My wife's mother used to tell her that her hair "looked like a cat sucked on it." This struck me as an odd thing to say, and it prompted me to ask some questions.

Where did this phrase come from? Was there just one specific hair-sucking incident from which the expression arose, or was there a period in time when cats went around sucking on everyone's hair? Did other people witness these occurrences? If so, what did they say? Did they say, "Excuse me, but there's a cat on your head, and I think, if I'm not mistaken, that it's sucking on your hair?"

Were the people whose hair was being sucked on aware of it? Or did they respond to the news that their hair was being sucked on by saying, "Oh really?" And then did they reach up and feel the top of their heads, only to find cats there?

I would think that something like this would have to happen often and would require several witnesses before it became a saying that was passed down from generation to generation.

Perhaps the expression arose from a time when animals behaved in ways that would be considered unacceptable in modern times. Maybe there was an age when hair-sucking cats were not uncommon. Maybe there was a Latin word for it like "catuslickushair."

Are there similar expressions out there that I am unaware of such as "Your clothes look like they were worn by a llama," or "Your face looks like a possum had it for a snack"?

Another question that occurred to me was, how can you tell, just by looking at someone's hair, that a specific animal had sucked on it? Does hair that was sucked on by a cat have a different quality, a different sheen, than hair that was sucked on by, shall we say, a dolphin?

As you can see, the phrase got me to thinking. I will continue to ponder it. Sadly, I don't have the answers to any of these questions now because, like they say, my brain feels like it was stolen by a rhesus monkey.

A Day Off

Robert and Nadine live in a resort community by the water. Sharron and I went to visit them because we thought that maybe we could do something there that we never do at home—relax.

When Sharron first mentioned the idea to me, I was surprised and confused. "Relax?" I said, "What's that?"

She tried to explain it to me. "It's when you don't sit at the computer writing, you don't work on the house, and you don't work on the yard. You just kick back with friends, talk and drink, and you don't really set out to *do* anything at all."

"People do that?" I asked.

"Yes," Sharron explained patiently. "Normal people do."

"Okay. Maybe we should give it a shot."

The day, for Robert and me, was to begin with golf. When I play golf, it isn't really relaxing, so I was fine with that. That way I couldn't claim that I had spent the whole day doing nothing. My god, what would people think?

The golf course is open to everyone who lives in the resort community, but, this time, there was a catch. There was a tournament going on. We were informed that we could get on the golf course if we wanted to, but we would have to wait for three hours. Instead, we opted to hit some balls at the driving range. There's a good chance that the golf gods had arranged this so that Robert and I would not damage the community's immaculate course. Normally, I suck at golf, but that day I would have extra sucked, if there is such a term. Maybe the word for it is suckified. I'm not sure, but you get the idea. My first ball went dribbling off the tee and landed about five feet in front of me. The second bounced across the driving range. The third angled off to the right, cutting across the view of the real golfers. I eventually got it under control, in the same way that someone might call an earthquake "under control" when it is just a tremor.

Robert and I agreed that the golf course was a safer place without us on it.

We went back to Robert and Nadine's and decided to go out on the boat. I had a beer, which is pretty rare for me at ten in the morning. On the boat, there were no computers, no weeds to pull, and in fact, nothing really for me to do except enjoy the scenery and the breeze coming off the water. I reluctantly gave in and did just that. I leaned against Sharron and smiled.

The bliss was eventually interrupted by a sudden sense of urgency and my immediate need to do something. My morning beer had struck! I informed Robert I had to use the facilities. We turned the boat around and headed back to the house. I began to feel good about my day. I had met with a crisis and resolved it. I was being productive!

But more leisure activities were in store. Next on the agenda was swimming. I was warned that the lake contained a certain amount of duck poo. Nadine told me to put on rubber slippers before I went in the water, and I asked her if this was because the bottom of the lake was slippery due to the duck problem or if there was some other reason.

"Do you really want to know?" she asked.

"Yes."

"Well, there are little worm things on the bottom of the lake that will stick to your feet if you don't wear the booties."

Nice, I thought. Worms and duck poo—a recipe for relaxation. But, regardless of this, the water was wonderful. Floating in the water beside my wife and friends, I again felt that unfamiliar feeling of actually enjoying myself. I knew subconsciously that eventually this would cause me to be eaten away by guilt (if not worms), but I was not going to worry about it just then.

Swimming was followed by a warm shower and another trip out on the boat where we had champagne, crackers, smoked salmon, and Brie. I ate all of it and part of a life jacket. Robert casually mentioned that when we got back to the house, we could do anything we wanted to, even fall asleep. I took note of this. Meanwhile, with the aid of the champagne and the serene blue waters of the lake, I reluctantly became comfortable again. There was some sort of calamity involving a missing champagne glass, but I ignored it.

It was about two in the afternoon when we returned to the house. I don't think Robert recalled mentioning that we could sleep, but I had recorded it in my mind the instant he said it, so I laid down on the couch and immediately passed out. There were Englebert Humperdink songs (Robert's choice) blasting on the stereo, but that didn't stop me.

I am told that while I was asleep, Robert, Nadine, and Sharron came over to look at me in wonder.

"He's asleep," they said.

"I can't believe he went to sleep."

Nor can I. Perhaps I had taken the whole relaxation thing too far, or maybe I was just getting good at it.

I don't know how much drama and intrigue you can stand, so I won't fill you in on the details of the rest of the day, except to say that we listened to loud music, talked, laughed, and had a great time, regardless of how against our nature that is.

We left, smiling and happy, promising that we would do it again sometime. But I thought to myself that it would be a while before we did. After all, having a great day like that just can't be good for you.

The Black Nine

Let's begin with a widely-known fact: Robert and I suck at golf. You don't have to remind us, though. We're fully aware of the situation. This is why we golf together. Our skill levels (zero and zero) are complimentary. During a round of golf, we can exchange such pleasantries as "Wow, Robert, that was almost as good as a normal person's shot," or "Gee, Bruce, if you had hit the ball that time, it would have gone a long way."

So we were chagrined when—on the first hole of the course we were playing in the Big Bear mountains of Southern California—a third person joined our friendly twosome. He was tall, muscular, and had just come off a successful run on the PGA senior tour, or so it seemed. Robert and I were grateful to see that he was walking the course while we were riding. This would give him something to do while Robert and I were making the extra shots necessary to catch up with him.

We were also disturbed by the fact that the course was well-monitored. There were course rangers and employees everywhere, although the most important type of course employee was absent—the beer cart lady. It must have been an oversight. There was no other explanation.

I'll not describe the details of our round for you—the triple bogeys, the topped balls, the tee shots that went no more than fifty yards—because I'm a kind person, and I want to spare you the pain. And, admittedly, I'm not sure I want to relive it.

We weren't there to play winning golf. We were there for exercise, camaraderie, and to see the wildlife. Robert had told me about the animals he had seen on the course the last time he played it, like the fox that sat, curled and watching, as Robert hit his driver from the elevated tee on the fifth hole.

But this time, things were different, and something odd happened. On the second hole, several birds flew overhead and made cackling noises, as if they had been closely observing my iron play.

On the third hole, they started circling, and they still sounded as if they were laughing. A hawk had joined them, and there were also a couple of ground squirrels on the sidelines. By the fifth hole, where Robert reported he had seen the fox, we had our own gallery of wildlife creatures. As I hit my fourth shot off the fairway, I swear I saw two of the ground squirrels pointing, holding their bellies, and laughing.

On the seventh hole, a short par three over water, I was glad that my ball landed in the sand trap because if it had landed in the water, I don't think I could have borne the ridicule I would have had to face from all the animals that had gathered around. At this point there were two deer, some rabbits, several squirrels, a full flock of birds, one hawk, three lizards, a snake, and a family of quail. They were obviously having a great time.

Now I know how Tiger Woods feels, although maybe it's a little different.

I made it out of the sand trap, and I believe I heard a smattering of applause from the squirrels, but I could have been mistaken. I might also be wrong to think that one of the deer let out a moan when I missed my putt for par. But who knows? Maybe the altitude was getting to me.

We finished our round and shook hands with the man who had joined us. We had learned along the way that he was the CEO of a local hospital. He said that, although he appreciated that we had let him join us, he would never hire anyone as clearly uncoordinated and incompetent as we were. Some of the woodland creatures cheered his name as he walked off the green. They had been joined by a large goose who added a chorus of honks.

"So what do you want to do now?" I asked Robert.

"Let's go hunting," he said, an evil grin on his face.

Oh, I knew he was joking. At least, I think he was. You never know with Robert.

We went and had a beer instead because that's what real sportsmen do.

Finding Things

When I look in the refrigerator, I see the items on the two shelves immediately in front of me. That's it. Everything else is a blur. It may come as no surprise, then, that I rarely find what I am looking for. There is something about the refrigerator that renders me helpless. I am suddenly incapable of moving a small jar of pickles to see what is behind it. I lose the ability to turn my head sideways, which would enable me to look at the shelves on the refrigerator door. These also, believe it or not, contain food items! Within several seconds of opening the refrigerator, I must call my wife for help.

"Oh please help me," I cry. "I am bewildered and confused."

I do not know what the solution to this problem is or even if there is a solution. When I was single, the refrigerator only contained three things: Ding Dongs, beer, and an orange. I could handle that, but it is not an option now.

I felt much better after I discovered that my wife has the same sort of tunnel vision and helplessness when dealing with paint cans.

We were in the garage working on a project, and she was standing in front of the shelf where all the paint is.

"Where's the green paint?" she asked.

It was right in front of her. There was green paint dribbling down the side of the can. The can itself was green. It said, "Green Paint" in big green letters. I didn't point any of these things out because I knew how my wife felt. If it had been a jar of pickle relish, I would have been unable to find it.

Finding stuff is hard to do. Before we leave for parties or any event where we have to be there at a specific time, my wife and I like to play a game. It involves ripping the house apart looking for something that we had previously put in an "easy to remember" location. Wallets and keys are perfect objects to search for in this game. To maintain domestic tranquility, we take turns on who loses them.

My favorite instance of this was when my wife and I were moving from one apartment to another, back in what we refer to as our traveling gypsy days. Everything in the apartment was in boxes. We were about to leave, when I realized that I didn't know where my glasses were. They weren't sitting on top of any boxes, and that's pretty much all that was left in the apartment. Thinking I might have dropped my glass case, we checked the ground outside. We checked the car and the truck. Then we began unpacking boxes based on the theory that maybe I had mistakenly packed my glasses. Forty-five minutes later, in hopes that my glasses might magically appear, we were checking in places where we had already looked twice before.

I was looking inside the toilet tank when my wife called me from the other room.

"Honey," she said.

"Yes," I responded, curious as to what she might have found.

"Remember earlier when you got something out of the refrigerator?"

Sure enough, I had left my glasses in the refrigerator. Maybe I subconsciously thought they would be helpful when I was looking for stuff there. Who knows?

As we were leaving for the new apartment (I was in a truck and she was in a car), I had to shout for my wife to wait up. When I had put my glasses on, they fogged over, and I couldn't see to drive. They were still ice cold.

After my glasses thawed out, we hit the road. I pulled up alongside my wife and asked, "Do you remember how to get there?"

"I'm sure we'll find it," she said. "Eventually."

A Taxing Situation

As I type these words I am currently on hold with the good folks who supply the product we'll call "Tax Frustration In a Box" or TFIB for short. My time on hold currently stands at twenty-five minutes.

I would like to tell you the story of how I wound up here, with my ear to the phone, waiting for a recorded voice to tell me to keep waiting. And so, I will.

It all started when we bought a house. I knew my days of filing 1040EZ were over. Complicated tax forms were one of the reasons I had avoided getting a house for so long. Of course there were other factors as well, like, for example, poverty.

When it came time to do our taxes after our first year of owning a house, we took our receipts, W2s, tax forms, and any other paperwork we had with numbers on it that we didn't understand to a gentleman we'll call Joe.

Joe was happy to do our taxes. He joked and laughed with us as he did. At one point, he casually mentioned some of the audits his business had undergone.

"Boy, I'm sure glad we don't have to worry about those anymore!" he exclaimed.

We solemnly nodded in agreement. I don't often look "askance" at people, but this was definitely an occasion when I did. I looked askance at my wife. She grimaced.

Our appointment with Joe was two months before the April deadline, but due to a clerical error on the part of his staff, we didn't receive the copies we needed to sign and send in until the day of April 15.

In life, I have found that, if I swear I am never going to do something, my chances of doing it automatically go up. Being a part of the mass of people who are running to the post office late on April 15 was one such thing. I swear I'll never do it again.

That experience prompted us to take another route with our taxes this year.

Let's return to the present. My wife just called down to me from the bedroom. "Are you still on hold?" she asked incredulously.

"Yes," I answered. The elapsed time is now thirty-five minutes. You are here, live, as it happens. Isn't this exciting?

Wait! The tech guy from TFIB just came on the line. His name is Nigel. He seems tense. Poor Nigel. He sounds like someone who has been harassed by people who have been on hold for long periods of time. No doubt, many of them were recently online and discovered that TFIB Inc. is having serious problems with its computer servers, making Internet support a virtual joke:

"Knock. Knock."

"Who's there?"

"Download Terminated, that's who!"

I had to take a break to work with Nigel, but I'm back. You'll be glad to know that I treated him nicely, and I did not call him any bad names. The only negative word used at all in our conversation was "squirrelly."

"It's a technical term," I said to Nigel.

"I know," he said. "I use it a lot myself. Really, I do."

We have a bond, Nigel and I. We both hate the company he works for.

Let's return to the painful and agonizing details of how I ended up doing our taxes on the computer. This year we decided to find someone else besides Joe Getyouaudited to do our taxes. We asked around. Our friends and acquaintances, who usually go berserk making recommendations for tax services, were strangely silent. It was as if they were all keeping their tax people a big secret. I am beginning to see why. A good tax person is a rare commodity. Finding one is like finding the donut with the white frosting and the chocolate sprinkles after all your coworkers have had their pick from the donut box.

We checked the phone book. We drove around. We passed a tumbledown shack that said "Pepe's Taxes" and kept on driving. We jotted down the phone number that was posted on a sign outside of someone's house. We threw it out when the owner of the house came outside in his undershirt to wave to us.

After much debate between me and myself (to which my wife patiently listened), we found ourselves standing inside a building that offered *professional* tax services. They have a logo that is in the shape of a green box, which, I figured out later, is symbolic of how your money looks when it is cut in half.

There were rows of desks in the building. Two of the desks were occupied by tax counselors working with clients. We stood in front of the reception desk. There was no one behind it.

It is one thing to be on hold for thirty minutes, but is another thing to be standing in a room, where people can see you, where it's obvious that you need help and are willing to pay money for it, and yet you are completely ignored.

Painfully reminded of my younger days spent in singles bars, I turned and walked out.

A half-hour later, driven by sheer desperation, we returned. The same two people were sitting at desks. One of them didn't have any clients. She ignored us. The guy, who had a client, got up from his seat and asked if he could help us. We told him we wanted to schedule an appointment, so he went to get the receptionist. The receptionist had been cleverly hidden away in the back of the building where she wouldn't have to be inconvenienced by helping people.

The room was quiet except for a series of smacking and popping sounds. The tax counselor who did not have a client was making the noises with her gum.

"Please God," I thought, "don't let her be the one to do our taxes." I had the feeling that I was looking askance again.

Like the Great and Powerful Oz from behind the curtain, the receptionist appeared to schedule our appointment.

"Monday around six would be good," I said.

"I'll put you down with Kim," the receptionist said, gesturing towards the gum-smacker. "She's really good."

Kim suddenly found our activities to be worthy of interest.

"Don't schedule those people at the same time that I have another appointment!" Kim shouted across the room. She punctuated it with a pop. "Rebecca did that to me the other day—scheduled two appointments at once! Can you believe that?"

"You know what?" I said to the receptionist. "Can you schedule us with somebody else?"

Kim strolled up to the desk. "Make sure you don't—smack!—put them down when I'm doing somebody else's taxes! Pop! I can't do more than one return at a time."

"They're scheduled with somebody else," the receptionist told her.

"Oh. Well. I can't believe that I was scheduled for two appointments at once!" The windows vibrated with Kim's voice. She popped her gum again. A dog outside barked at the noise.

I asked about the price, gulped upon hearing the answer, and left quickly.

In the car, I turned to my wife. "So honey, will you call and cancel tomorrow, or do you want me to cancel?"

"I'll do it," she said.

Which is how we ended up using the TFIB software. You'll be glad to know that Nigel, only minutes ago, solved my problem with his company's squirrelly software and, as I type this, our state return is printing out on our new computer that we claimed depreciation on.

There is one catch, though. Electronic filing and the state software, which are advertised on the TFIB package as free, are only "free" if you submit rebate forms. Yes, that's correct, as a result of buying software to help you fill out forms, you have to…fill out more forms. Personally, I'm not sure how to do them. Tomorrow, I'll go find someone who can help me.

Hey, maybe there's software for it!

Champions on Crack

Ladies and Gentlemen, he's the winner of no gold, silver, or bronze medals! When he wears ice skates, he looks like a bowlegged cowboy. He's your host for this column: Bruuuce Smith!

Hi folks, sorry about the introduction. I've been announcing everything that way ever since my wife and I went to see *Champions on Ice* at the Anaheim Pond. The Anaheim Pond, as those of you who are residents of Southern California may know, is not a pond at all, but an arena. We went to see this ice-skating extravaganza because we got free tickets. I am the kind of ungrateful bastard who can get something for free and still make fun of it, so I have to mention that the seats were in the nosebleed section. From where we sat, miles above the arena, we could see very famous ice skaters, whom I had never heard of before, spin around on the ice. They were all very eager to demonstrate how limber they were, especially the female skaters who did moves you can't get away with in public, but that are perfectly acceptable in the middle of a crowded arena. Music played and lights flashed. The two girls behind us screamed like we were at a Beatles concert back in the 60s.

The screams were loud and shrill. My wife began to bleed from her ear.

"Do you think the bleeding is caused by the screams or by the elevation?" I asked her.

"What?" she said.

The two screaming girls were at *Champions on Ice* with their parents. Their parents kept telling them to shut up.

"Shut up yourself," one of the girls said to her dad, making me grateful once again for that vasectomy I had years ago.

Just so you don't think I live in a festering sinkhole of negativity, I'm going to say something positive. The ice skaters were very good. There, I did it.

I said to my wife, "You know, watching these young performers demonstrate their athletic skills makes me want to go sit down and have a big dinner."

Occasionally one of the skaters, as part of his or her act, would leave a piece of clothing on the ice. I noticed that during the performance, instead of thinking thoughts like, *Wow, that was an awesome three-point twirl*, I obsessed over the fact that clothing was still laying out on the ice. I found myself thinking, *I sure hope she picks up that jacket. Somebody's going to trip over that thing!*

It seems that I have reached entirely new levels of compulsiveness. I could get a gold medal in it. If only they had an Obsessive/Compulsive Olympics:

"We join competitor Bruce Smith as he lines up the tape dispenser and the stapler on his desk for the third time today."

"It's amazing, John. Have you noticed how he quadruple checks everything he does?"

"You're right and…wait! It seems that Mr. Smith has pulled a ruler out of his desk. He's using it to line up his sticky notes!"

"I've never seen anything like it! Let's see what scores the judges give him."

My favorite part of *Champions on Ice* was during the intermission when the machine came out and cleaned up all those messy ice shavings. I was able to see this because I was in and out of the men's restroom in about two seconds. My wife, on the other hand, is still in line for the women's restroom, and I miss her very much.

My second favorite part of the show was the music, an interesting mix that included Louie Armstrong, The Scorpions, and Prince. Ice skating is more like dance than it is like wild game hunting—a *lot* more. The routines were varied and diverse. They were the most un-routine routines I have ever seen: a girl twirled Hula-Hoops while skating; a guy stood on a bald man's head while wearing ice skates, and another man shot and killed a gazelle. That last one I made up, but the other two were for real, so, as you can tell, it was pretty interesting.

As the show progressed, the unusual acts grew more frequent, and the show became increasingly surreal. In one sequence, they used a very strange lighting effect that was never explained. It made the ice look like it was covered with eyeballs. I took my glasses off, cleaned the lenses, and put my glasses back on. The scene hadn't changed. People were still skating on eyeballs.

Perhaps this was meant to prepare us for the finale in which the whole thing just got out of hand. The finale was an odd, garish, circus style performance set to Spanish music. There was lots of orange—the color, I'm told, of insanity. A line of male skaters, dressed like matadors, glided across the ice and waved their capes around. Female skaters zipped by them and twirled. Strange poles were moved around the ice, seemingly at random. They were decorated so that they sort of looked like lollipops, but it wasn't clear what they were actually supposed to be. They weren't *definitively* anything.

What is happening here? I wondered.

Some guy, dressed like a clown, maybe a jester, stood in the middle for a minute while the lollipop sticks were moved around again. Another guy, who was dressed like something I can only describe as "a fluffy tree," skated to the edge of the ice and wiggled his legs at our part of the audience. Chaos reigned. Suddenly I was at *Champions on Crack*.

It was a barrage of the unexpected, but we knew it was the finale because that's how the show ended. The skaters bowed. We, the audience, recovered from our dazed state and applauded. I left the auditorium, saw my wife in line for the bathroom and told her to call me, then made my way out to the car.

On the way home, it occurred to me that my column is a lot like *Champions on Ice*. It often starts off normal and gets increasingly bizarre. Realizing this, I pulled off to the side of the road, turned my radio to a Spanish station, climbed up on my car, and did a hat dance.

"Arriba! Arriba!" I yelled.

I bowed to the passing cars, and people threw roses to me, causing me to trip and fall onto the curb, where I lay uninjured, but happy to have entertained my fans.

You can applaud now. It's over.

Medieval Dimes

My sister made us an offer we couldn't refuse; if we would drive her and her husband to Medieval Times, they would pay for the tickets. I leapt at the chance, having always wanted to go.

We arrived at Medieval Times an hour early because traffic was better than expected, so we went to the bar and had a round of drinks. From where I sat, I could see a small courtyard through the windows and a sign that said, "Dung." I couldn't see all of the sign, but I extrapolated that the full sign said, "Dungeon." Either that or it had something to do with all the horses in the show.

My brother-in-law told us that we would walk through the courtyard once we had purchased our tickets. "Don't be surprised if they try and sell you things," he said.

When we saw people begin to filter through the courtyard, we went outside and got in line for tickets. We were immediately handed a paper that said that if we paid a little extra, we could get front row seating, a banner to wave, a special dessert, a foot massage, and a date with the Medieval Times employee of our choice. These tickets were $5000 each and were available for purchase straight ahead. Otherwise, tickets were only $4500 each. To get those, you had to go up the stairs to the left, make your way through a leech-invested swamp, walk through a labyrinth, and escape from a dragon that shot flames at you. We chose this option. At the ticket counter, we were told that we could buy tickets to the dungeon, where we could view various devices of torture. This would cost $200 apiece.

"No thanks," I said. "Being a creative spirit trapped in an incredibly tedious nine-to-five job, I am already familiar with torture in its many varied forms."

The lady at the ticket counter pretended to ignore me.

Tickets in hand, we were directed to a woman who unceremoniously placed paper crowns on our heads. She told us that we were to cheer for the knight whose colors were on our crowns—in this case, the black and white knight. You could even call him a "checkered" knight and talk about his checkered past if you wanted to, but I'm not sure why anyone would want to do that.

We then had our first photo opportunity of many, in which we could have our pictures taken with a princess. To avoid this and the accompanying $800 fee, we had to walk between the camera and the princess herself. Past the courtyard and inside the lobby, we could get our picture taken as we were knighted by the King. Price: $1400. We declined.

The lobby led directly into the gift shop where there were medieval costumes, chessboards, T-shirts, goblets, jewelry, and postcards. You could also buy the one and only original sword "Excalibur" that was given to young King Arthur by the Lady of the Lake and wielded in many legendary battles. It was on sale for a paltry three billion dollars. They had twenty of them.

Lining the gift shop were horse stalls. The horses, it turns out, are the stars of the first half of the Medieval Times show. These Andalusion stallions are proud creatures, magnificently groomed, and royal in demeanor. They also bite, which explained why glass had been put up between their outdoor stalls and the gift shop. Still, the stallions were elegant, and I considered going back to have my picture taken just to make sure they were well fed.

Right before we were let into the arena, it was explained that there were six different knights in the show. Each section of the audience would be cheering for their respective knight. We were seated based on the color of our crowns.

Once seated, we were greeted by our serving wench. (We were instructed to use that chauvinistic term, so get off me.) Our big-breasted wench also described dinner and told us that, if we didn't know it already, we would be eating with our bare hands.

The lights dimmed, mist filled the arena, and the crowd cheered rambunctiously. From the voiceover that accompanied the introductory music, we learned that the King and his knights had won a war, and we were there to celebrate their victory by enjoying a feast and watching a tournament. It was the perfect setup.

As we were introduced to the characters of the show, including the horses and the knights (we gave a rousing cheer to ours), our food was brought out. The serving operation was a well-oiled machine. Dinner was timed to go along perfectly with the show. The servers were working their butts off. Two of the servers didn't even *have* butts anymore.

I had some reservations about eating soup, chicken, a pork rib, and a potato with my bare hands, but except for a certain amount of greasiness, it was a surprisingly decent experience. Meanwhile our knight was doing quite well in the tournament. Our section kept chanting, "Black and White! Black and White!" I lost interest in the tournament only once, when I knew dessert was coming. While everyone else yelled, "Black and White!" I yelled, "Pastry! Pastry!" My loyalties almost always lie with my stomach.

As we finished our meal, the servers brought us warm wet cloths to wash our hands with. The cloths weren't quite enough to do the job. I felt like I had chicken smeared all over my face, on my arms up to my elbows, and possibly in my undershorts. My sister, being a loyal and devoted member of the Royal Order of Towelette Collectors, had brought along moist towelettes that she passed out to our little group. I gave her a big thumbs up.

Shortly after dinner ended, some announcements were made about birthdays, anniversaries, bachelor parties, graduations, and bar mitzvahs—all of which were being celebrated that night. My sister told me that she would have had them announce my birthday, but it cost $100. I told her that the moist towelette was good enough for me.

Once dinner was over, the show picked up pace. Now was the time for hawkers to try and sell us banners and light sticks while photographers tried to take more pictures of us. As this was going on, the tournament continued below. Knights charged each other on horseback, and people charged things on their credit cards. The knights swung swords and battle-axes at each other. Checking accounts became overdrawn. Sparks flew as the weapons collided. We flinched as weapons bounced off the knights' shields. My stomach rumbled because I had eaten both my chicken and half of my wife's. If I were one of the knights in the show, I would have burned off my meal with horseback riding and athletic stunt work, but I wasn't. I just kicked back and let the fat cells form.

The music during the show was also great, but most everyone was so caught up in the action that they didn't notice. Afterwards, I told my wife and my sister that I was going to go to the gift shop and pay $150 for the soundtrack. They both said, "Soundtrack! There was music?"

The lady at the gift shop asked if I wanted to buy the DVD as well. I looked at the price.

"Maybe when I become CEO of my own company or when I inherit millions of dollars from an unknown uncle, then I will be able to afford the DVD," I said.

"Perhaps, sir," she responded, "a cassette tape would better fit your economic status."

"Touché," I said and paid for the CD.

It's a great soundtrack, by the way. I play it at home while I eat buckets of fried chicken and play Dungeons and Dragons on my computer in an effort to somehow recapture the Medieval Times experience. I do this because, despite the costs (I may have mentioned them), it was great fun.

I can best summarize it this way:

Tickets to Medieval Times: $4500

Drinks and souvenirs at Medieval Times: $380

The Medieval Times experience: Priceless

High-speed Incompetence

We live only blocks away from a Starbucks and a movie theater with stadium seating, so it came as a surprise when I discovered that, according to a wide variety of telephone and cable companies, we still live in Podunk.

I was trying to find someone who provided high-speed Internet service in our area, but I was learning that barely anyone did. "I'm sorry, sir," one lady said. "Your area is too rural. You may be able to get your tractor repaired locally, but you'll never get DSL. Maybe you should go back to your crops and forget about it."

I hung up my cell phone, had my android assistant bring me another drink, and tried another company.

The end result of my phone calls was that there was only one outfit (as they say out here in the boonies) that provided service to our area, a company called "Cheater." Cheater was eager to provide us with high-speed Internet. They also wanted to replace our cable service and our phone service with their own. I wasn't interested in either of these, especially since it had taken months to get our cable service to work correctly, and we were now functioning under the axiom that (like my grandpappy used to say when we talked about getting an indoor toilet) "If it ain't broke, don't fix it."

I set up an appointment for Saturday, between eight and noon, to have high-speed Internet installed. Throughout the week, we had several people call to confirm that, yes, we did have an appointment for Saturday, and—oh, by the way—were we interested in their cable TV and phone services? We counted a total of six calls, and that's without exaggerating.

Saturday came, and at one o'clock that afternoon, after no one had arrived, my wife called Cheater and asked them what was going on. I speculated that the mule they use to deliver things in our area had broken a leg.

The lady that my wife talked to said that she needed to talk to me. Their conversation went like this:

> "You'll have to have your husband call us to resolve this problem."
>
> "He's right here."
>
> "You'll have to have your husband call us to resolve this problem."
>
> "He's right here."
>
> "You'll have to have your husband call us to resolve this problem."
>
> "He's right here."

My wife handed the phone to me.

"It's really important that you call instead of your wife," the lady told me in a robotic voice not unlike that of my android assistant whom, incidentally, my wife had sent off for a couple more drinks. She had given him the instructions, "Less Seven Up, more vodka."

After setting up my wife as an authorized caller, I was allowed to deal with our real problem—that our service man was a no show. The lady from Cheater responded by telling us that a technician was still available in our area and that we should stay at home and wait for him. I made the wacky suggestion that perhaps she could call the local installation service, ask what the delay was, and ask when the technician would arrive. Maybe the service could even get back to us with that information.

"We'll send them a form," the lady said. "We'll send them a form every hour if we have to. Stay where you are."

We did as ordered.

At four forty-five that evening, the man from the local installation service called and told us that several people had called in sick. He asked if we would like to reschedule. My wife and I debated the issue and decided to go for it, but we weren't sure it was a good idea. Working with the people at Cheater had proven to be more time-consuming and aggravating than downloading megabytes of content from a graphic-intensive Web site via a dialup modem running on Windows 98. Which, I might add, is pretty frustrating.

We rescheduled for the following Saturday between eight and noon. When the day arrived, I was relieved to see the service technician at two o'clock in the afternoon. My wife had left to go shopping for a carrier pigeon so that she had a way to quickly send messages to her friends. I had just gotten off the phone with Cheater, who had called me to ask if I was interested in any of their other services. I believe I said, "Are you kidding me? I can't even get this one installed!"

Our technician was an okay guy, although he was a tad bit forgetful. After he had installed the service and gotten into his truck to go to his next stop, I found a bag of cable connectors he had left in our garage. I ran them out to him, and he thanked me. As he drove away, I felt pretty good about myself. Then I saw that the installer had left the check I had given him on the floor of the computer room. The switch inside that changes me from being a good person to a bad person flipped over to the dark side. I didn't call anyone. I just set the check aside.

Later that night, the technician called us because he couldn't find the check in his paperwork. I told him he could pick it up anytime he wanted. I would leave it at the side of the house, hidden under a pile of cow manure.

So now we have high-speed Internet, and it's a wonderful thing. I can send my wife instant messages telling her how much I love her while she's sitting only three feet away from me in the computer room. We can play poker over the Internet without having to go through all the trouble of taking those pesky playing cards and chips out of the closet and setting them up at the dinner table. It's great. I just love technology. Don't you?

The Renaissance Unfair

Renaissance Fairs are popular in many locations throughout the United States. However, not everyone has heard of the Renaissance Unfair, an event designed for the single purpose of illustrating the lesson that life is not fair.

The Renaissance Unfair is open to everyone. Rich people can get in for a piece of cardboard or a wad of gum, whereas the cost of admission for those on welfare is $7500.

If you're wondering what kind of attractions one might find at the Unfair, I have provided descriptions of several of them below:

> Jousting: A knight on a stallion does battle with a midget, who is armed with a twig and rides a three-legged mule. I can hear the sounds of it now: the blaring of trumpets, the pounding of hooves across the ground, a thud, and a mild smattering of applause.

The "Good Things Happen to Good People" Fun House: While making your way through the mirror maze at the start of this attraction, a team of psychiatrists monitor your behavior to determine whether you are basically a good person. If you are *not* a good person, you can get through the fun house in approximately two minutes. If you are a good person, the floor will drop out from under you; you'll land in a room where you are spun around until nauseated, and then you'll be beaten with rubber clubs. As a finale, a clown will spray you down with a firehose while yelling, "You get what you deserve!"

Games: Every fair has its midway. The Renaissance Unfair has Rip-off Row. Rip-off Row features games of chance under banners that say, "Lose Your Money Here!" "The Odds Are Against You!" and "Go Home Broke and Miserable!" It works in Vegas, why not here?

The "Everything that Goes Around Comes Around" Merry-go-round: People who believe that life is fair are fond of saying, "Everything that goes around comes around." This ride is designed to dispel the belief by not allowing anyone to make a full circuit. You get on; it goes about three-fourths of the way around, and the ride operators throw you off. As a final punctuation to the lesson, the ride operators will often yell, "Ha!" when you land, face first, in the dirt. The line for this attraction is an hour and a half long and taking cuts is permitted.

News on the Big Screen: Still believe that life is fair? Enter the "News Theater" where you can watch network news on a hundred-foot tall movie screen. The presentation is in Dolby Surround Sound. No pregnant women, people with back problems, or small children are allowed.

Psychics: The palm readers tell everyone that his or her lucky number is nineteen and a half, but the last time it will ever be lucky was last week. The tarot card readers tell all the married people that they will soon meet the lover of their dreams.

Those who leave the Renaissance Unfair still certain that life is fair, that karma works, and that justice will always be served, will find happiness in their denial. Those who get the message are punished for their intelligence by having to live with the harsh truths of reality.

Doesn't seem fair, does it?

DeodoRant

The label on my deodorant says that it "goes on clear" and is "invisible." I find it necessary to point out that "white" is neither clear nor invisible. If you paint your face white, does that make you invisible? No. It makes you more obvious, unless, of course, you are standing in a room full of mimes. Did the invisible man paint himself white? No! If that's all there was to being invisible, then there'd be a lot more bank robberies. Obviously, to the manufacturers of my deodorant, the difference between opaque and transparent isn't very clear. Oh look, I made a pun!

Maybe what the manufacturers mean is that deodorant is invisible because no one can see it when you're wearing it under your clothes. But, even then, it's not invisible. It's just out of sight. But hey, I'm not one to quibble.

What kills me is that the "invisible" deodorants are actually more noticeable—more visible—than your regular "visible" deodorants. They might as well be glittery and fluorescent. They are, in fact, anti-invisible deodorants being marketed as invisible deodorants.

Wait! I just figured it out. It's the advertisers' *motives* that are transparent. There, that's one mystery solved.

Now I have to figure out the whole odorless concept. Frankly, I think the idea of something being unscented just totally stinks. I imagine this conversation:

> Jan: Here. Smell this.
>
> Tommy (sniffing): I don't smell anything.
>
> Jan: I know. It's odorless!
>
> Tommy: Then why did you have me smell it?
>
> Jan: So you could see what it doesn't smell like.
>
> Tommy: You're insane. Please seek professional help.

While we're on the subject of advertising, if it says, "easy installation" on an item's packaging, you should know, right from the start, that you are being lied to. The only exception to this that I can think of is my deodorant, which also makes this claim. I figure they knew they couldn't make good on the whole "invisible" thing, so they thought they could make up for it by stating something they were sure they could pull off. This got me to wondering if there might be a situation in which deodorant "installation" wouldn't be easy, and it occurred to me that it would be difficult for a one-armed man. But then again, a one-armed man would only have to wear half the deodorant, so maybe it balances out. I'm not sure.

Regardless, if they're going to market the deodorant for all of the above reasons, they might as well advertise it as "noiseless" too. "Tired of having important meetings disrupted by your noisy armpits? Stop the embarrassment now! Buy our new silent deodorant! We promise; it won't make a sound."

Another option is to come up with a series of deodorants with names like "Sweaty Man," "Woman Who Had a Stressful Interview and Then Jogged Several Miles," or the generic "Smells like B.O.!" They could be odorless and invisible, yet still live up to their names! Here's another one: Water Reclamation Plant.

Heck, if they wanted, they could put bad jokes on the labels (I could write them), and then they could market the deodorants under the brand name PUN (Personal Underarm Neutralizer). "The next time you need to make a pit stop, use PUN!"

I'll start pushing this idea as soon as my other products hit the market. For the record, those products include no-hold hairspray "for that windblown look" and transparent makeup—marketed with the slogan "All that work for nothing."

I don't see why there should be any difficulty selling my new products. My idea for jeans that look like they've already been worn was a big hit.

You know that guy who sold the emperor the invisible clothes? I think he was onto something.

Still Running

Our toilet wouldn't stop running. It was like some mad racer who, after crossing the finish line, continued to run, leaving all the others behind as they sweated, gasped for air, and worked off the leg cramps. Like the proverbial Timex, the Energizer Bunny, and some of the blabbermouths I've known, it would not stop. I asked it to. I asked nicely. But it refused to see the logic of my arguments.

"Aren't you tired, Mr. Toilet?" I asked. "Aren't you exhausted from running and running and running? Give yourself a break. Relax. Chill. Or, if you'd like, just knock it the hell off!"

The toilet stopped making noise for a second, as if considering these words, and then the slow hissing and bubbling of water started right up again.

What to do? I looked my problem up on the Internet and found this helpful advice: "Do not talk to your toilet or take it to counseling. Although your toilet does need professional help, a certified psychotherapist will do little good. Instead you should call a professional of a different nature—a professional who charges just as much as someone with a PhD, but who isn't afraid to get his hands dirty. These people are called 'plumbers.'"

I had heard of plumbers before, but I was too proud to use them. No, I would fix the problem myself. (Could this be anything but the foreshadowing of doom?)

In order to fix the toilet, I had to turn the water off first. The problem is, the water at our house doesn't turn off. The main valve that leads to the house turns, but it only slows the water. It never completely brings it to a halt. It's like a bad crossing guard that can't keep people from crossing the street or a goalie who can't stop the ball. It's like a columnist who can't prevent himself from making a stream of analogies.

I tried to turn the water off at the street and discovered that I didn't have the right tools to do it. At this point in the story, those of you poor demented souls who are familiar with plumbing will ask the question, "Why didn't you just turn the water off at the angle valve adjacent to the toilet?"

Well, Mr. Smarty Pants, I didn't do this because some idiot had installed a straight valve instead of an angle valve, and I wanted to fix that too. Especially because, if a real plumber ever did come to our house, he would figure out that it was me who installed the straight valve.

Unable to turn the water off elsewhere, I gave up replacing the valve and decided just to fix the toilet itself. Opening up the tank revealed that an oil spill, or some other environmental catastrophe, had taken place in the back of our toilet. The black rubber parts in the tank were so old that they had started to fall apart, decompose, and do all the sorts of things that dead things do. It was what the professionals call "yucky." Cleaning that up, I thought, would be a job for the wife.

But before that could happen, I had to remove the tank. With my head stuck between the bathtub and the side of the toilet bowl, I ask my wife if she could hand me the vomit wrench. You might think that I intended to say "crescent wrench," but "vomit wrench" is truly what I meant. The reason it's called this is because all my tools were at one time stored in a toolbox that my father gave me. My father, for the entirety of my life, never gave me a single thing that was brand new, even though, reportedly, he could afford to. He always gave me old, secondhand, cheap crap. The toolbox was one of these items, and before he gave it to me, he kept it in a leaky old shed, and the toolbox rusted. Being the handyman that I am, the toolbox sat untouched in my closet for several years. When I finally opened it up, it smelled as if someone had upchucked into the toolbox and sealed it shut. The tools that were in it still retain the stench. As a result, when I asked for the "vomit" wrench, my wife knew exactly which one I was talking about.

The wrench didn't work. The nuts and bolts that held the tank in place were so badly corroded that they wouldn't let go. They were like starfish super-glued to a rock in a tide pool. They had the death grip of a clingy lover who won't give you any space and makes you so intensely claustrophobic that you think you might just go mad. They were on there good.

What I needed was a socket wrench (which is vastly different from the dirty sock wrench my father gave me). This was the perfect excuse to run out and go shopping, possibly for tools. We headed to Kmart. There were so many interesting things there, like DVDs and Playstation games, that we were completely distracted from our task. We might have picked up a socket wrench, but I don't even remember. All I know is, we never fixed the toilet.

Now, whenever we pass by the bathroom, we routinely walk in and jiggle the handle. It's like we're shaking hands with it. "Hello Mr. Toilet. How are you today?"

"I'm just fine," it will gurgle. "Now leave me alone."

And that, my friends, is where our story ends without ending. It goes on and on and on, like an impudent and unrestrained toilet, which is like a whole bunch of other things.

Dating Myself

Today I'd like to talk about the time I dated myself. I'm not talking about when I told a group of people that I was still trying to transfer all of my old 45s onto an IPOD, and nobody knew what 45s were; I'm talking about the time I actually took myself out for dinner and a movie.

The date started off well enough. I picked myself up right on time, which is easy to do because I know where I live. For dinner, I chose a fine local restaurant where I ordered a cheeseburger, and he ordered a patty melt. The food was great, and at one point during the meal, I caught him eyeing my food. I knew what he was thinking.

Conversation was kind of weird, though. Sure, we had a lot in common, but he kept saying, "Been there, done that!" It kind of put a damper on things. Fortunately, I have a good sense of humor, and I handled it well.

When he got up to go to the bathroom, I went with him. I know that's kind of unusual for us guys, but that night I was breaking a lot of rules.

The waitress took good care of us, though. "Have a good evening you two," she said as we left the restaurant.

She treated us like a couple. I assume she heard me talking to myself.

When we got to the movies, there was a bit of tension because he wanted to see a comedy, and I wanted to see an action film. We compromised and decided on a comedy action flick, but then there was a debate over who was going to pay. Ultimately, I gave in and let him buy the tickets, but only because he was so insistent. Heck, he was beside himself.

During the show, he got cold because of the air conditioning, so I loaned him my jacket. I wasn't using it anyway. *Maybe that'll score me some points*, I thought, but he acted like it was no big deal, as if I give my coat to myself every day! I even let him share my Coke and popcorn, which is something I don't do for just anybody.

After the movie, of course, I drove him home. The date ended pleasantly enough, but there was no good night kiss, not even a hug goodbye. When I got home seconds later, I figured it was over, and that was the last time I'd be seeing myself. But wouldn't you know it, the very next day, I heard from myself again. I guess I was lonely.

Over the following weeks, I was seen in public with myself on several occasions, but, surprisingly, the tabloids never made anything of it.

Eventually the relationship vanished as if it had never existed. Not too long after that, I dated a woman.

Actually, I carbon dated her. I just wanted to find out how old she was.

"You could have just asked me!" she said.

I don't know why she was so upset; I wouldn't have minded if it was me. I asked myself, and he told me so. At least *he* understood me.

I guess I should have expected all this. They had warned me that the dating scene was a whole different world. I just never realized how true it was until I experienced it myself. And with myself.

Thank goodness that was years ago. Every day now, I thank the stars that I met my wife. She saved me from all that insanity.

Plan B

Plan A was to sit and watch Stargate DVDs all evening. Plan A is always subject to change. Its very existence was threatened by the various chores that lay around the house waiting to be done. But then the wife introduced Plan B, which was to go to the store and buy some sheets. Plan A died and went to the Planet of Plan A, which is where all Plan A's go when they are not carried out. I sometimes imagine a huge plain on the Planet of Plan A where Plan A's roam about looking for something to do. It is a purgatory of sorts, from which Plan A's can sometimes be retrieved. My personal plan was sent there for a week's stay. My personal plan was on the purgatory plain on the Planet of Plan A.

So off to the store we went.

There were two parts to Plan B. Part one was to buy the sheets. We pulled this off with incredible precision. Any male of the "hunt, kill, and return home" mindset would have been pleased. Part two of Plan B was to return home immediately and put the sheets on the bed so that we didn't have to wash the old ones.

"We cannot live one more day without new sheets on the bed," my wife had said.

I cannot blame anyone but myself for the failure of part two of Plan B. Part two of Plan B was predestined for failure, so that it would ultimately wind up in the province of purgatory on the Planet of Plan A's reserved for partially performed portions of Plan B's.

The rest of the evening was spent in direct avoidance of ever returning home where, we suspected, there was work lurking in every corner waiting to leap upon us. Some of the work I had left undone in the yard was now, I believed, physically capable of doing this. As were some of the things we had left in the refrigerator.

Impulse buying took over, and we spent a large amount of time and money in Borders bookstore. We didn't have any money, but we try never to let that be a deterrent.

Hungry after all of our spending, we went to the International House of Pancakes where you can have pancakes any time of day without being mocked by your waitress. This portion of our home-avoidance technique was somewhat marred by the unpleasantness of the group in the next booth, two grandparents and their grandson. I guessed, from the looks of it, that they had been sitting in the booth for quite some time. They appeared to be stuck.

"As long as we're trapped here," they may have said to each other (I am only surmising), "let's have some more pancakes."

I doubt that I would have noticed them if it were not for their conversation, which consisted of the grandmother screeching the words "Don't kick me" at her grandson. It was timed at irregular intervals, like drops of water in a Chinese water torture session. Just when we had forgotten about it and begun to enjoy our meal, the words would come again, "Stop kicking me!"

It was said in such a way that one wanted to directly disobey the person issuing the command. Maybe that's why it persisted. I offered to go over and kick the woman myself. My wife, in her wisdom, deflected my attention back towards my pancakes.

We finished our meal and left IHOP. Thankfully, I had only ordered the short stack. Otherwise, I might have been stuck there too.

On the way home, between us and the chores that awaited us there, was a movie theater. We found a movie that was rated WA for Work Avoidance, which meant that it probably wouldn't be very good, but it was perfect for people who had papers to grade and weeds to pull.

We got home late that evening, locked the garage, locked the downstairs door, shut off all the lights, turned on the alarm, went upstairs, looked at the bed, and remembered that the sheets were in the trunk of the car.

We looked at each other and laughed. We said something like "Forget it!" and went to sleep.

A week later, I was watching my Stargate collector's edition DVDs, and the crew of SG1 went through a wormhole to find a planet where unfinished plans go. They found my Plan A and returned it to me where I sat. So the story has a happy ending. Just thought you should know.

Nuttysystems

"What just died?" I asked my wife. I rounded the corner into kitchen and saw that Sharron was unloading a box of Nuttysystems food.

I stopped in my tracks. Had I offended her? Had I just undermined her new diet plans?

I lucked out this time because she looked like she was about to gag. "Maybe," she speculated, "it will smell better after it's cooked."

Initially, when she had told me about the Nuttysystems plan, I thought it was a good idea. They send you your meals. You eat 'em. That's it.

Supposedly, the meals are based on something called the Glycemic Index. I first learned about the Glycemic Index when I saw a book called *The Glucose Revolution*. The book was sitting on a coworker's desk. The title brought to mind an image of a bunch of glucose taking over a government by force and installing its own leader. "Viva la Revolucion de Glucose!"

This turned out to be an incorrect impression.

What's the big deal with glucose anyway? I wondered. When I heard that some people were glucose intolerant,

I thought that meant they went around making derisive comments about glucose like "Glucose sucks!" and "I hate glucose!" Crazy anti-glucose people.

My coworker tried to explain it all to me, but I wasn't really in the mood for anything technical. Silly and stupid was pretty much my mindset.

"The Glycemic Index," my coworker said.

"The blah, blah, blah," I heard.

"…is a ranking of food based on how quickly the carbohydrates in it are digested."

"Blah, blah. Food. Blah, blah, blah, blah."

She handed me her copy of *The Glucose Revolution*, and something in it caught my eye. What I found interesting (okay, amusing) was that the authors of the book—men and women with PhDs who should know better—were referring to the Glycemic Index by its initials, G.I. In common medical parlance, G.I. stands for gastro intestinal, which makes these initials very useful to someone like me whose mind sometimes sinks to a near, if not sub, childlike level.

Thus, G.I. Joe becomes Gastro Intestinal Joe. Instead of blowing things up with a hand grenade, he blows them up with his butt. To use a term from *The Glucose Revolution*, a meal consisting of bean dip and chips would be considered "high G.I.," as well as being a highly effective tool in G.I. Joe's arsenal.

Another example: Where I work, the distribution department refers to the processing of a shipment as the Goods Issue. Often, just for fun, when they tell me that the G.I. has been issued, I will say, "Upper or lower?"

To which they will either say, "Huh?" or "Ha ha. You are such a child, Bruce. Why don't you grow up?"

When my wife and I sat down with plates of Nuttysystems food in front of us, we discovered that G.I. actually stands for "Grossly Inferior." The food tasted like plastic. Sour plastic. Sour, slightly alien plastic that makes you queasy. With just a hint of cheese.

We tried several times, but we couldn't get it down. Maybe that's the real secret to the diet, we theorized. The food tastes so bad that you just don't eat.

We wrote it off as one of those failed experiments that you learn from. Either way, I hope that you, too, have found this to be educational, and I also hope that you have enjoyed today's highly sophisticated discussion of science. Because that's what I'm here to do. I'm here to inform. Next time, I'll be talking about stem cell research and why I think it is unnecessarily cruel to plants.

X-Rayted

When the doctor told me that a normal rheumatoid factor is under fourteen, but that mine was seventy-three, I was impressed with my score. I thought, *Wow, for someone who's just a beginner, I'm pretty good at this arthritis thing.*

My doctor referred me to a specialist and told me that I should bring the x-rays that had been done by my company's worker's comp clinic. "It should be no problem at all," he said. "In fact, they're legally required to give them to you." Whenever someone tells me that there shouldn't be any problem, this sends up a red flag that a problem will probably occur, so I braced myself for the inevitable.

My first impression of the clinic, when I initially had the x-rays done, wasn't too favorable. On that visit, I learned more about the receptionist's personal problems than I did about my medical condition. I hoped for better the second time around and attempted to make it as pleasant as possible by calling ahead and asking what I had to do to get my x-rays. The man who answered the phone said that all I had to do was come in and fill out a form.

I arrived early Monday morning and was greeted by a new receptionist whose expression reminded of a fish that had washed up dead on shore due to mercury poisoning. Apparently, no one had told the doctors in the office that one of their own was in desperate need of help. Slack jawed and glassy eyed, the receptionist referred me to a gentleman who asked if I had gotten my company's permission to pick up the x-rays. My answer was "No." So he called them and asked if he could give me the x-rays. They said yes.

At that point, it would seem that the next obvious step would be to hand me the x-rays and, maybe, a release form. The man behind the counter handed me several sheets of paper and said, enthusiastically, "Here you go!" He acted as if he had given me my x-rays, so that I could go merrily on my way to happy doctor land. Using all the powers of observation at my disposal, I was able to point out that the papers he had given me were a description of what the clinic's doctors had said about the x-rays, but they were *not* the actual x-rays themselves. I was able to tell this because they were not pictures of *bones*.

"Oh, we can't give those out," the man said. "The x-rays are our only records of treatment. If your doctor can send us a release form, we will send him the x-rays directly."

Let me take a brief moment to say that there are certain things in this world that I do not like. I don't like asparagus. I don't like ongoing physical pain. I don't like it when I'm misinformed. And I don't like it when people "handle" me in some cheap "customer service" kind of manipulative way. And while I'm at it, I also don't like anchovies.

But I also know that sometimes the best way to win in this type of bureaucratic game is to follow along through all the wacky steps, get it done, and then make fun of everyone afterwards. From a passive aggressive point of view, it's a stroke of genius!

I took my pseudo x-rays, took a deep breath, and went to work. From there, I called the office of the arthritis specialist, Dr. Calamari. Calamari isn't his real name, but it's close enough for important medical records. I asked the receptionist if they could order the x-rays from the industrial clinic. Sure they could, she told me. All I'd have to do was come in and fill out the release form. "I'm surprised the clinic didn't tell you that," the receptionist said.

Here's the deal. When she told me this, it was nine o'clock on a Monday morning. Yet I already felt as if I had endured an entire week of bureaucratic ridiculousness. Now, I had tunnel vision. I no longer cared about anything else, or felt emotionally capable of dealing with anything else, except getting those x-rays where they belonged. It was my mission—my single, solitary goal in life. I took some sick time, drove thirty minutes to the doctor's office, and filled out the freakin' #%&!! form. Twice.

The form was a little ambiguous. I was surprised that the receptionist hadn't told me that. For some reason, I thought that I was the one "receiving the health information." But no, that's the doctor. So I guess, in a few days, Dr. Calamari will be receiving some x-rays along with an explanation telling him that he has arthritis.

I, oh so politely, turned in the second form, and then drove, quietly and serenely, home. It is there that I now sit, typing this with a smile on my face. Oh sure, with every letter I type, my joints get stiffer and the pain gets sharper, but as the Buddha said, life is suffering. And, clearly, the people running the front desks at certain medical centers are trying to teach us that if you can't get rid of the pain, you might as well embrace it.

Medicalitis

In a recent column, I outlined some of the problems I had obtaining x-rays for an upcoming doctor visit. It will probably come as little surprise, to those of you who are familiar with how our world works, that when I finally did have the appointment, nobody had any clue as to what had happened to the x-rays, and I had to get a new set done. This I did willingly because the alternative was to go back to work and be productive.

The x-ray tech assigned to me was suffering from a disease I have seen evidence of before—a psychological illness known as ILS, which is short for Inappropriate Laughter Syndrome. This occurs when a person repeatedly says things that aren't funny and then bursts out laughing as if she had said the cleverest thing in the world. My past experience with this particular ailment enabled me to diagnose it quickly. The problem is that when you first come in contact with this disease, and you don't know that someone has it, the initial reaction is to wonder, *What is wrong with me? Why aren't I laughing? Are there jokes here of such subtlety and magnificence that I am just too dense to get them?* The answers to these questions are that you are just fine and that the person you are dealing with has a serious mental condition. Once the x-rays were finished and I knew I had done my part to better my own health, I hoped, against all probability, that the x-ray tech would follow suit and go see a shrink.

Getting x-rays was the first of three things the doctor recommended. The second was getting more blood work done, and I am happy to report that everything went perfectly well there. The staff was wonderful and friendly, and the blood was eager to get out of my body and into the little vials, like rats leaving a sinking ship.

The last thing on the list was to pick up my prescription. This too, went well. But sadly, when things go well, it's not very funny and makes for a boring column. In some future column, I will describe a series of events in which everything went just as it should, and you will never finish reading it because you will have fallen asleep long before you ever reached the end. "Where's the dramatic tension?" you'll ask. "Where's the conflict?" And then you'll wake up to find that you have dozed off and fallen asleep with your face in your soup. Or you might have a nice little dream in which aliens are trying to sell you farm animals. There are all kinds of things that can happen when you fall asleep, and almost all of them are more interesting than a day that's going well.

Lucky for you, the medication the doctor prescribed for me had side effects. This is the case for all drugs I take. Before I take them, I might as well take the list of possible side effects and circle one at random, just so I'm prepared to deal with something weird. The drug prescribed this time might as well have been called "Bathroomidan." I suspect that the drug is secretly manufactured by the good people at Charmin, just so they can bring in a little extra cash.

This was decidedly confirmed on my second day of taking the drug, which is about the time that I discovered a bruise on my arm from the blood work the day before. I realized that everything there had not gone as well as I had perceived. Now that I think about it, the lady who took my blood did seem kind of angry.

At this point you're probably wondering, *where does this all take us? Why do I even care about Bruce Smith's medical problems?*

I don't have the answers to these questions. But what I've learned from the medical profession is that this is okay! You don't have to have the answers. You can just keep experimenting and doing tests, and you still get paid! How convenient is that? So, see the receptionist on the way out, and she'll set up an appointment for next month. Meanwhile, take care of yourself.

A Sinking Feeling

"Nice vanity cabinet you have there," one of our guests said, referring to the four-by-fours that held up our bathroom sink.

"Thanks," I said.

"Wasn't it like that last Christmas?"

"Yeah," I acknowledged. "It's been that way for a year and a half now."

It was a sad, sad truth. Since one of the lines to the faucet sprung a leak, and we tore out the old vanity cabinet, which had been saturated with water, there has been nothing there except for the four-by-fours and a square of bare concrete. It wasn't that we hadn't tried to replace the cabinet. My wife and I spent hours in the major hardware stores looking for just the right one. Like Goldilocks, we had become a bit picky: "That cabinet is too big. That cabinet is too small. That cabinet would be just right if it didn't cost more than a recreational vehicle."

The decision became overwhelming, and so we consulted a number of sources. The last source was a

Magic Eight Ball, which gave us the cryptic and rarely seen message, "Are you kidding me?"

This gave us no option but to do what we are best at—procrastinating. We are "pros" at crastinating because we are better at it than others are. We call *those* people "amateurcrastinaters."

Once we finally did venture out and find a vanity cabinet, it sat in our dining room for a week until we unpacked it. After all, we are pros at this crastinating stuff. When we did open it up, we found that there was a problem. Between the two doors in the front of the cabinet there was a quarter-inch space like the gap in a hillbilly's teeth. The manufacturer had put the hinges on wrong. I was aggravated that the vanity had been assembled poorly, but I knew better than to take it out on the cabinet. It seems that both the cabinet and I were starting to become unhinged.

"Why does there always have to be some kind of problem?" my wife asked.

"Oh," I said, "You must be thinking that we live in the tolerable universe. That's the universe next door. You and me, we live here in the crazy, messed up universe."

She didn't find this to be the least bit helpful.

As I stared at the vanity cabinet trying to rationalize a way to keep it and not send it back (which I knew, deep in my heart, was futile), she got on the phone and spoke to the manager of the hardware store. My wife hadn't originally intended on talking to the manager, but the store hung up on her twice, and the third time around, talking to the manager seemed like the appropriate thing to do.

I tried to demonstrate to my wife what was happening by using visual aids. I held out my left hand and bunched it up into a ball. "See this? This is the good universe, where things usually go right. Now this," I said, holding out my other hand, "is our universe, which is wacky and uncooperative. You can't get from one to the other. We're stuck here."

She wasn't paying attention. The manager on the other end of the phone had begun fumbling his way through an attempt at figuring out how to start to begin to go about solving our problem.

I didn't hear the full conversation. I just got a general impression of it from what my wife said and from her facial expressions (mainly a lot of grimacing and eye rolling). But here's what I made of the conversation from my side: The manager had absolutely no idea what to do. He was going to go to a management training class on how to solve this kind of problem and call us back when he had completed the course. Again, this may not be how the conversation actually transpired.

My wife hung up. We returned to the vanity cabinet, lowered the box back over it, and taped it up for transport back to the hardware store.

"Well," she said, "you're off the hook."

She was right! Suddenly a ray of sunshine pierced the grayness of gloom and frustration that had begun to overtake me. Today was going to be a better day than I had anticipated. I wasn't going to have to hold a wrench! I wasn't even going to have to work with tools! I was free! Free to live! Suddenly, and only for a moment, I felt as if I lived in the best of all possible universes.

"Hey," my wife added, "you wanna go shop for cars?"

Tired

Changing tires makes me hungry, not only because of the physical exertion, but because the tires look like donuts. They look like those big Hostess donuts that are covered in dark chocolate.

My mouth watered as I swapped the big tire from my car with the small spare.

Yum. Yum. I thought. *If only they actually made donuts that size.*

Between my hunger pangs and a lot of lifting and cranking, I managed to get the tire changed. Then I made my way to, uh, BigMart, where I had bought it not too long before.

"What was wrong with the tire?" I asked the mechanic when they were all done.

He told me that the seal along the rim had broken. That meant nothing to me. He might as well have told me the tire was clinically depressed.

"By the way," the mechanic added, "I wouldn't trust that spare very long. It has teeth marks on it!"

"Oh, that's nothing to worry about," I said sheepishly, quickly exiting to the parking lot.

When I got out to my car, I noticed that a hubcap was missing, so I walked back over to the shop and asked the mechanic about it. He told me the car only had three hubcaps when I brought it in. I had him double check the shop to make sure. With no hubcaps to be found, I assumed I must have lost it on the freeway.

A month later, I got another flat on the same tire and returned to BigMart.

They told me to leave the car for an hour and to go into the store and spend as much money as I possibly could. This is the beauty of the BigMart tire warranty program.

I filled up a shopping cart as instructed and returned to the tire center an hour later to find that they hadn't done anything at all to my car.

"We've been trying to contact you," the guy at the counter said. "You need a new tire, and we don't have that tire in stock."

"How did you try to contact me?" I asked. I was carrying my cell phone, and that was the number they had.

"Telegraph," the guy explained. "It's more reliable than cell phones."

"I see. So what's the deal with the tire?"

"We don't have it."

This led to one of those awkward customer service moments where I stood there waiting for the guy to say something customer service-like, such as "We're sorry we have been incompetent. Please wait while we call a nearby store and see if they have a tire in stock."

Silence.

There were three people in the tire center at the time because it was in the process of shutting down for the day, and that's apparently when all the employees show up. None of them seemed to understand why I was still standing there.

Fortunately, the manager of the department arrived and offered four possible solutions:

1) Try calling other stores in the area and see if they have the tire in stock.

2) Order a tire. It would take a week until they got it in.

3) Come back tomorrow when the next shipment of tires was due to arrive and see if, by chance, the tire I needed was in the shipment. If I chose this option, the manager said, they would take my name and phone number and call me when the tires came in.

4) Buy a new car that matches the tires they have in stock.

Option 1 didn't work. I passed on option 2. I seriously considered option 4 and then reverted back to option 3. Like the naive girl who just dated the class jock, I told them that I would be waiting for their call the next day; then I paid for my stuff and went back to my car. When I opened up the trunk, I saw that not only had they given me my tire back, they had also given me the hubcap from someone else's car (true story).

"I see how this works," I said.

When BigMart didn't call the next day, I returned—out of sheer curiosity more than anything else—to see if they had gotten the tire in. They had not. A day later, I had my tire replaced at the family-owned brake shop down the street.

Several days after that, there was a knock at my door. I opened it to be greeted by a man from Western Union.

"Mr. Smith?"

"Yes?"

"Telegram for you."

I signed for it and opened it up. It said, "MR. SMITH. STOP. WE DO NOT HAVE TIRE. STOP. PLEASE STOP SHOPPING. STOP. COME BACK TO SERVICE DESK. STOP."

That was going to be the punch line to my story, but of course, there really wasn't a telegram from Western Union, and truth is stranger than fiction. A week after my adventures at BigMart, their service manager left a message on the answering machine telling me that my tire was in.

I told my wife that the tire, which I never ordered, had arrived.

"Wow," she said. "Now that's customer service!"

Your Receipt

Thanks for shopping at BigMart Shopping Center and Pharmacy.
This is your receipt!
Merchant ID: JASABAZADOODOO9

=+=+=+=+=+=+=+=+=+=+=

BIGMART! WHERE EVERY DEAL IS A BARGAIN!

=+=+=+=+=+=+=+=+=+=+=

You were served by: Bob Darmott, employee #4212562018596046198, badge #1388721032120015. If you have any personal beefs with Bob Darmott, he can be found at his home address: 2099 Baycliff Ave.

=+=+=+=+=+=+=+=+=+=+=

Please bring this receipt with you if you wish to return your product. This receipt is in no way a guarantee that you will receive your money back, and we reserve the right to change, alter, or lie about any part of this receipt that we so choose. Customer service representatives are authorized to grab this receipt from your hands and then deny that you ever presented it to them.

=+=+=+=+=+=+=+=+=+=

BIGMART! WHERE EVERY TIME YOU VISIT IS WHEN YOU SHOP HERE!

=+=+=+=+=+=+=+=+=+=

Please cut out and save this portion of your receipt to receive a $5.00 discount on the new bestselling album *Hamsters of Anarchy*. Coupon is redeemable only at this location on Thursday evenings after five in the late fall months, which are determined solely at our discretion.

=+=+=+=+=+=+=+=+=+=

BIGMART! WHERE WHAT YOU SPEND IS THE PRICE YOU PAY!

=+=+=+=+=+=+=+=+=+=

Our marketing executives are so desperate for your feedback that they will award you big money, cash prizes, and/or nothing if you visit us at www.BigMart. com and participate in a short twenty-five minute survey. Please be advised that none of the questions asked will be relevant to the things you find most annoying about our store, and you will never get a chance to express those sentiments to anyone who can do something about it.

=+=+=+=+=+=+=+=+=+=+=

BIGMART! WHERE YOUR EXPERIENCE IS WHAT HAPPENS TO YOU!

=+=+=+=+=+=+=+=+=+=+=

BigMart is committed to keeping our environment green. As a result, we offer this nature-friendly suggestion: Please do not throw out your receipt! It can be recycled in many creative ways. You can use it as a blindfold or, if you move it three inches upwards, a funny headband. Receipts for purchases over $100 are long enough that they can be wrapped around empty toilet paper rolls and used for personal hygiene. Or, if you like, there is enough room on the backside of one of our receipts for you to write an entire novel, including several appendixes.

=+=+=+=+=+=+=+=+=+=+=

BIGMART! WHERE SAVING MORE WILL COST YOU LESS!

=+=+=+=+=+=+=+=+=+=+=

Again, thank you for shopping at BigMart! We know you have many other choices, some of which are vastly superior, so we are extremely grateful that you went slumming and came to our store. Please honor us with your presence again. We so greatly appreciate your business that we are willing to do anything for you except for teaching our employees basic social skills. Please return as soon as humanly possible. If you leave the store, get out to your car, and realize that you have forgotten something, we recommend immediately turning around and coming back inside. At that time, you will undoubtedly indulge in some more impulse buying. If impulse buying is a problem for you, please call 1-900-GET-POOR, and you will be connected with a counselor who can help relieve the guilt you feel over your spending problem. (Calls are $2.50 per minute for the first three minutes and $7.00 a minute thereafter. Additional fees may apply.)

=+=+=+=+=+=+=+=+=+=+=

Your fortune for today:
HAPPY SMILES WILL BRING YOU PEACEFUL
PROSPERITY

=+=+=+=+=+=+=+=+=+=+=

Oh yeah, your purchase total was: $4.98.

Your total savings for today were: $0.00.

Your balance was paid with: Credit Card, Cash, Check, or Personal Favor.
(Note to employees: please circle one.)

A gratuity has been included in the cost of your items.

=+=+=+=+=+=+=+=+=+=+=

Copies of this receipt are also available in German, Spanish, Hungarian, and French.
Customer agrees to all terms and conditions regardless of whether they know such terms and conditions exist.
No purchase necessary.
You may obtain receipts for products you did not buy at www.BigMart.com.
For official rules to an imaginary contest that no real person will actually ever win, please visit www.BigMart.com.
To earn rewards, work hard in life and don't expect some store to give them to you. It's not our responsibility.
Couldn't find what you were looking for? Tough!
For questions, please call 1-900-GET-LOST.

Have a nice day!

Customer Copy
Receipt #73186510.324
Ticket #8
Password that will allow you into official CIA records:
I82MUCH
Random meaningless code: #$AK:fow1e;oa
APPROVED

PLEASE SAVE THIS RECEIPT FOR YOUR
RECORDS
(PREFERABLY IN A THREE-RING BINDER)

Dividing by Zero

At work the other day, this guy came up to me and asked, "What do you get when you divide by zero?"

Thinking he was joking, I answered, "I don't know, a brain hemorrhage?"

He said, "No, seriously."

"Well," I said, "you don't get anything because you can't divide by zero."

"That's not right," he said and walked away. I thought perhaps I had misunderstood him, but I listened as he asked someone else the exact same question. Then he began explaining how it could be done.

Dividing by zero isn't possible because you need something to divide with. Saying that you are going to divide by zero is like saying that you are going to slice up a birthday cake but you have lost the knife. The only difference is that with an uncut birthday cake you end up with a bunch of whining children, and when you try to divide by zero, it's just me who whines.

Let's take the following sentence and break it down: "We are going to divide by zero."

"We are going to"—A bunch of us got together to perform an activity.

"divide"—The thing we are going to do is divide.

"by zero."—But we chickened out.

They tell you that you should "choose your battles." *This* is my kind of battle—a quarrel over an entirely insignificant issue that I should just leave alone.

I walked over to the cubicle where my coworker was performing his numerical magic, hoping that I could help him see the error of his ways.

Before I said anything, I stopped and listened as he explained division by zero to another cubicle dweller. I was surprised to find that divide-by-zero guy was getting results. Like "five." It was a stunning achievement.

When he was through, I tried to explain to him, as I have explained to you, that you can't divide by zero. He let me get clear through my presentation, but I must have left out some key point because he stared blankly at me for a second and then restated his explanation exactly as before. Normally this is when I resort to name-calling, but, instead, I turned to the person he had been talking to and demonstrated that if you *multiplied* two times two, you got a totally different result than you would if you *added* two plus two. What the hell. If you can't beat 'em…

The next day the divide-by-zero guy got a job in accounting. They heard he was good at manipulating numbers. I suspect he'll have a 200 percent accuracy rate.

Five Sides to Every Story

Some time after the divide-by-zero incident, I had a similar experience.

A guy in the office gave me a list of questions designed to test observational skills. The quiz had questions about objects that you see every day. The questions were like, "What color is at the top of a stop light, red or green?"

Another question was, "How many sides does a stop sign have?"

"Eight," I answered.

"Nope," said the guy who had handed me the test. "There are five."

Now, I was pretty sure about this one, but, still, I'm one to check my facts. That evening, I looked at all the stop signs I passed on the way home, and each one of them had eight sides.

The next day at work, I confronted my friend and said, "You know, I looked at several stop signs, and they all had eight sides."

"No, you're wrong," he said. "Count again."

I took a pencil to paper, and I drew a stop sign for him.

"You're drawing it wrong," he said.

Another person looked over my shoulder and added his commentary. "No, a stop sign is longer than that. There aren't that many sides." My friend walked away with a smug look on his face. I swear to you this really happened.

The quiz-giver's sense of authority and conviction left me questioning myself. Had I counted wrong? Maybe I was in a hurry driving home.

There was no way I was going to leave this alone, so I went to my dictionary and looked up "stop sign." It said, "A stop sign is a red octagonal-shaped piece of metal with a white outline and the word STOP painted in the middle. The stop sign is used as a traffic control device in many parts of the United States. If the word octagonal is too big for you, it means, having *eight* sides. 'Oct' meaning *eight*, as in 'Octopussy,' the character in the James Bond movie who slept with James Bond *eight* times. If anybody challenges you on this, be sure to make a big deal out of it." That's what it said, right there in Webster's.

I went around the office and verified with several people that a stop sign does have eight sides. Even though they agreed with me, most of the people I asked gave me a funny look, as if they were wondering what I was up to.

Back at my computer, I printed a clipart picture of a stop sign and numbered the sides one through eight. I carried it over to my number-challenged friend, showed it to him, and said, "What am I missing here?"

He looked at it with a puzzled expression and then said, "Oh, you're right. I must have been thinking of something else."

I felt as if there was nothing else to say to him, except, maybe, "What else? What in the hell else could you get confused with a stop sign!" So I went around the office and made fun of him behind his back.

That was until somebody pointed out to me that stop signs do indeed have five sides: the left side, the right side, the inside, the outside, and the outside peripheral edge. Once again, I had been proven wrong, and it was ultimately my arrogance and my own narrow worldview that had brought me down. So I went to Mr. I-Failed-Geometry and apologized to him, telling him that street signs could have as many sides as he wanted, that I was very sorry, and that I would never, ever, question him again. I had foolishly assumed that I could decide things based on facts, when I should have realized that the truth is subjective. It's based on perception, and anyone's opinion is just as legitimate as someone else's. How could I have been so blind? How silly of me.

The Shape of Things

I was working on a project that involved geometric shapes, and I realized that I did not know what a seven-sided shape was called. Research revealed that it has two names: septagon and heptagon. Heptagon has superseded septagon in recent usage, but I found it interesting that there were two sides to the seven-sided shape. Perhaps this is to make up for the fact that this often-overlooked shape hardly gets any press. You hear about hexagons and triangles all the time, but meanwhile the poor little heptagon is silently being exiled. I was a little bent out of shape about it, so I thought that maybe I should start campaigning for the rights of the seven-sided shape.

These days, whenever I get a totally nonsensical idea, I check the Internet to see who else has had it. I found a site for an organization called the Committee for Recognition and Acceptance of the Septagon and Heptagon. I thought it would be a cinch to join CRASH (as they call themselves) but it was more difficult than I thought. They had membership dues, and you weren't allowed to pay with credit cards, checks, or bills that were rectangular in shape, nor were you allowed to pay with coins that were circular. (It would be hypocritical.) I overcame the payment obstacle using Origami and some oddly shaped gold doubloons. I was also required to take a class on the seven-sided shape, but it was over pretty fast because it was a CRASH course.

In my studies, I found out that "sept" is the prefix for seven, which made me wonder why the ninth month is called September. Turns out there are two reasons for this. September is so named because it was the seventh month of the ancient Roman year, which began with March. In addition, the seventh month had already been named July in honor of the Roman goddess Julie, who spent her days talking on the phone.

While I'm on the subject, do you know what would be a great name for a month? Number. It would be perfect for one of the winter months because they're so cold that if you're already numb, they make you number.

Meanwhile, as long as there is no month named Number, you can still pretend there is and use it to avoid meetings. Say that someone wants to schedule a meeting with you, and you don't feel like going to it. Just suggest that you meet on Number 17, and while they're trying to figure it out, you can sneak away. Or you could just say, "I don't want to have a meeting." It's up to you.

I would continue making up goofy things, but the representative from Triangles United is here to see me. We were supposed to meet on Number 3, but he rescheduled.

The Doctor

Remember the old TV show *Lost in Space* and the subsequent movie remake? I was reminded of that when I went to the doctor recently.

I was never really fond of the show as a kid because the conniving, sniveling, bad person in it was named Doctor Smith, and the other kids would make fun of me because my name is Smith. I tried to explain to them that, in real life, doctors aren't conniving, sniveling, and bad; that's just the people who run the HMOs.

My doctor's name is Doctor Mama. He has a business card that says, "Every doctor's a mama and so is Doctor Mama." It's like a riddle or something.

Regardless, I'm not really fond of my doctor because he's obsessed with my weight, which I assured him would be a lot less if I lived on the moon. (I was still thinking about space, you see.)

At a convention recently, I heard a gentleman give a talk about the expanding earth. My doctor is always talking about my expanding girth.

"If you continue at this rate," the doctor told me, "you will soon be as big as Jupiter."

In my head I had visions of that floppy-armed robot saying, "Danger, Will Robinson! Danger! Danger!" I'm not sure if the warning was because of potential cardiovascular problems or if it was because the doctor was about to give me the exercise speech.

I cut him off before he even got a chance. "Doc, I don't have time to lose weight. In order to lose weight, I would have to get up in the morning and exercise. Then on my breaks at work, I would have to go for walks. I'd have to do overtime to make up for all the time I spent socializing, which I would have done on my breaks except for the fact that I was walking. The money from the overtime wouldn't help me because it would go towards my health club fees. Then when I got home, I'd have to cook my own food because fast food is fattening, plus I'd have to go to the store everyday to buy fresh food and vegetables because they go bad so fast. Whatever time is left would be spent looking for my vitamins! I don't have time!"

Doctor Mama was eager to change the subject after that, so we began talking about some of the new markings and appendages that have recently appeared on my person.

"What's the red bulbous thing on my leg here?" I asked, fearing the worst.

He looked at it carefully.

"It's a bump," he concluded.

I assumed that was the medical term. "What's it from?" I asked.

"Age," he said. "You're getting old."

"You know," I said, "if we were in China, you'd say that with a little more respect."

He stared at me.

"What's this thing then?" I asked, pointing at a mark on my shoulder blade.

"It's a tattoo."

"No it's not, Doc," I argued. "I would have remembered getting a tattoo!" I looked at it in the mirror. The mark was big and said, "Becky." I don't even know anybody by that name.

"Let me see," he said, examining it again. "Oh, you're right. That's just a blemish."

"All right then. Can you identify *this* protuberance? I never had this before."

"That's your stomach," he said.

"Oh."

On the way out of the office, I asked, "Hey, uh, Doc, why didn't anyone warn me that my body would get like this when I got old?"

"Would you have believed it?"

"No."

"That's why. Oh and, by the way, according to your blood tests, you're a Martian."

"Thanks!" I said smiling. Finally, I had a real problem I could tell people about. I was happy.

The Dentist

As a humor columnist, it is obligatory that, at some time during my life, I write about going to the dentist. Up until this point, I haven't done so because I have the best dentist in the world—in the real world, that is. If I had the best dentist in the imaginary world, then he would talk to me for a couple minutes, announce that my teeth were perfect, and pay me a hundred dollars just for visiting. I would also get a balloon and a *Bullwinkle and Rocky* toothbrush kit. But that's just me.

What makes my dentist so good in the real world is that he both talks and listens to his patients. He is not from the Megalomaniac School of Doctoring and Dentistry (MSDD), which teaches that patients know nothing about their own problems and that they shouldn't be allowed to ask any questions about them either.

It was in a conversation with my dentist about a pain on the driver's side of my mouth (my terminology, not his) that he decided I should go to a specialist. There was a possibility that I might need (insert dramatic music here) a root canal. If the words "root canal" do to you what they do to me, then you might want to go and put on some Depends before finishing this column.

I showed up at the specialist early in the morning. The first thing that I noticed was his diploma hanging on the wall. He had a degree from MSDD.

I call him Dr. Whatshisname because I only saw his face once. Dr. Whatshisname asked me a few questions so that he could ignore what I was talking about. I asked him a couple of questions, but getting answers from him was like, well…pulling teeth.

He went about figuring things out for himself, which he accomplished by poking metal things in my mouth and spraying ice-cold water around until he found a spot where it hurt. Don't get me wrong. He was very good at this part. He found the painful spot very quickly.

I immediately shot up through the roof and out past the Earth's atmosphere, where I got a great view of the Northern Hemisphere. Then I bounced off the moon, shot back through space, and landed (very precisely) in the dental chair. The doctor was waiting for me with these words: "You need a root canal. We'll get started as soon as the receptionist discusses financing with you."

Like me, you may have heard that root canals are terribly painful. It turns out that the really painful part is the financing. I knew I was in trouble when the receptionist asked if I was a homeowner. Fortunately, I have insurance, so I'll be able to eat in a couple months, which works out fine because that neatly coincides with when my jaw will stop aching.

I found out from the doctor's aides, who were allowed to talk to me as long as the doctor wasn't around, that the procedure would take two visits. They handed me a paper explaining what is involved in a root canal because MSDD graduates are expressly forbidden to ever explain anything to their patients. I won't share the explanation with you because, frankly, it's not something you want to read about.

A friend of mine says that whenever he gets his teeth worked on, he tries to imagine that he's a rhinoceros on the African Savannah with his mouth wide open and that there are those little cleaning birds picking at his teeth. I tried to imagine the same thing, except it seemed that my birds had needles, drills, sledgehammers, and other instruments that birds should not be allowed to use.

The specialist did the work and, two weeks later, I went back for more because I enjoyed it so much. When the doctor finished, he ran quickly out of the room. The doctor's aide raised my chair and announced that I was done.

I looked to see where the doctor had gone. "Who was that masked man?" I asked.

"I don't know," the aide answered. "The doctor called in sick today."

I nearly leapt out of my chair. "What?!"

The aide laughed. "Just kidding!"

Didn't she know that *I'm* supposed to be the comedian?

Now that it's over, I know that I have faced one of my worst fears. I have put something on my credit card without knowing how I would ever be able to pay for it.

I can't wait to get back to my real dentist. We'll have a little chat, he'll dig around in my mouth for a bit, and maybe, just for fun, I'll let him put in a filling. It'll be a piece of cake, which, now that I mention it, sounds kind of good.

But yes, I'll floss when I'm done.

Phased Out

Much to his dismay, I have been seeing my doctor more often. On my last visit, he had the nerve to ask me if I had been watching my weight.

"Yeah," I said. "I've been watching it go up!"

Weight gain was a side effect of one of the medications he had prescribed. The label on the prescription bottle says, "Side effects may include, but are not limited to: death, bleeding eyeballs, diarrhea or water retention (whichever comes first), ingrown toenails, growth of unexpected appendages, allergies to all the foods you like, scraped knees, excessive foot tapping, inability to stay awake during long meetings, increased sensitivity to rap music, poor dental hygiene, irrational phobias, trouble with your in-laws, wedgies, involuntary spitting, recollections of past lives, existential angst, and in your case, weight gain. Do not use this medication if you intend to operate anything heavier than a fork."

I don't feel guilty complaining about medical problems because doing so is a constitutionally provided right for all people over the age of forty. If you are over sixty, it is no longer just your right; it is your duty. I took it up on the day of my fortieth birthday, but I have always tried to keep it interesting. Eventually, I plan to have a series of puppet shows about my health problems.

In preparation, I have begun cataloguing the phases of growing old, along with the related symptoms. They are listed below. Keep in mind that these are only generalizations and may only apply to me. Your actual experiences may be worse.

Phase 1:

- Going jogging results in a five-pound weight gain.

- You make pop culture references and discover that the things you are talking about are no longer part of pop culture. You also discover that some of the people around you weren't even alive when the first Star Wars movie came out.

- When people tell you that you're still young, you suspect them of trickery.

Phase 2:

- You feel like you partied all night when, in actuality, all you did was watch TV and go to bed at eight.

- When you go to the doctor, dentist, or optometrist, they are no longer able to help you with your problems. They used to fix them. Now all they do is say, "Sorry! That's what happens when you get old."

- Suddenly, and for no apparent reason, you stop caring about what's cool. The next day, you start making fun of it.

Phase 3:

- Every time you wake up, you discover a new wrinkle, crack, line, spot, or blotch. You figure out that if you never sleep, then maybe they won't appear. It takes so much effort to figure this out that you decide to take a nap.

- Words, which previously had no meaning to you, now mean something—words like Metamucil.

- In the middle of the night, your body parts get together and draw straws to determine which one is going to hurt the next day. Defying the odds, several of them get the short straw.

Phase 4:

(Please note that the elements of Phase 4 are not things that have actually happened to me yet, but by extrapolating from current trends, I have concluded that they probably will happen to all of us):

- Time goes so fast that the rest of your life takes place in what feels like an hour and a half.

- You find that acting stupid is a great way to mess with young people.

- You gain ten pounds that will not go away regardless of what you do. Two pounds of this is ear hair.

"Doc," I said as I left the office, "I'll be back." He didn't think I caught it, but I saw him roll his eyes. Poor guy. He doesn't know what he's in for.

The Candle Gang

I'm driving towards the freeway, and in the old beat-up car in front of me are two of the meanest, baddest looking guys I have ever seen. Their windows are rolled down and they are glaring out at the world with intense hatred. But their license plate frame says, "Partylite—Do You Love Candles?"

I burst out laughing. When I pull up next to them, I resist the urge to yell, "Hey! Do you guys have any lavender-scented candles? I need some for the doilies on my end tables," and "How about peach? That would go really well with the curtains in our guest bathroom."

Instead, I turn my head away and suppress my giggles. I don't want to make them mad. They might drive me off the road and force me, at gunpoint, to buy a box of candles. That would be robbery, but then, based on the checks I've seen my wife write out for candle parties, it's always robbery. Talk about organized crime.

All this is based on the assumption that the license plate frame belongs to the guys in the car. Maybe they stole the car, or it could belong to one of their girlfriends. But wouldn't that be great if they really were selling candles? If drugs were legalized, it could happen. Gangs would turn to selling Tupperware and candles because of the extreme profit margin.

"Yo Boy, wassup?

"Hey man, I got some fine product here."

"You messin? Like what?"

"Cucumber, bro. The subtle fragrance of cucumber candles."

"Sweet. Gotta get me a piece of that."

"Right on. Tell your homies."

What if one of the abovementioned thugs met a girl named Maria who sold a rival product line, dooming their love before it ever began and leading to a tragedy of Shakespearean proportions? I can see it now: the Westside Wicks versus "The Tupps." They'd perform amazing dance moves, waving lighted candles in each other's faces and snapping Tupperware lids to demonstrate that airtight grip:

"When you're a Wick,

You're a Wick all the way,

From your first candle sale

To your last day of pay."

Enter the Scrappers. You may not want to scrap with them, but you may not have a choice. If they don't get booked by the police, then you might get booked by them. That's right; with their paper cutters and their fancy backings, these hoodlums take scrapbooking to a whole new level. Truly a sales force to be reckoned with.

The light changes, and I return to reality.

I can't resist. I turn to the guys in the car beside me and yell, "See ya girls!" Then I peel out and zip onto the freeway onramp. Several seconds later I check my rearview mirror. There's no one there. Whew. Maybe they thought twice about messing with me. After all, I'm crazy. Plus, I've got a trunk full of fabric paints, and I'm not afraid to use 'em.

That's a Medium?

We live in a society where words are often misused. Today's examples come to us courtesy of the fast-food industry. I am speaking of drink sizes.

For example, small no longer means small; it means tiny—so tiny that you can get dehydrated while drinking it. Medium no longer means medium; it means "bigger than a house." Your options are to either get a Coke the size of a shot glass or a Coke the size of a Sparkletts water bottle. It's your choice.

To say it a more colorful way, a guy can either get enough liquid to enable him to write his name in the snow or he can get enough liquid to enable him to write the names of everyone in his area code in the snow—a virtual yellow pages, if you will. Nor is the price difference proportional. There is a ten-cent difference between the two.

I mentioned this to a guy at a fast-food restaurant I went to recently, but he was too busy to answer or to take my order. He was trying to get the phone number of the girl who worked the French fry machine.

Standing there with nothing to do, I ruminated on the fact that I couldn't get a medium if I wanted to because medium means extra large, extra large means gigantic, and small means "barely enough to be detected by an electron microscope."

The guy who was supposed to be serving me went on break, and the girl at the French fry machine went to the lobby to rub a dirty rag on some clean tables.

I went next door.

The place next door offered a regular drink and a large drink.

I failed to look at the menu and ordered a small.

"We don't have a small," the lady said.

"But I'd like a small."

"You can get a small next door, sir."

"No, I can't. I tried. I guess I'll take a medium."

"Do you mean a regular, sir?"

I ordered a regular, but thought to myself that "regular" was a meaningless term in a world where none of the drink sizes are standard.

The regular turned out to be extra large.

After a survey of various restaurants, I discovered the following: A store that has medium drinks is in no way required to have small drinks. Some places have a "mystery" medium drink that is only available in certain meals, but not separately. And if you super-size your meal, you will get a huge-jumbo-mega-large-bonus drink.

Also, when you order a small drink, it usually comes with the straw from the huge-jumbo-mega-large-bonus drink, which, proportionately, will make you look like you are trying to suck the life out of a drink the size of a marshmallow. (Not that there's anything wrong with that.)

A similar problem, which can cause even further long-range difficulties, occurs with hot sauce. Some of the varieties available include Mild, Regular, Spicy, Hot, Extra Spicy, Burn Your Lips Off, Burn Your Neighbor's Lips Off, and Fry Your Hypothalamus. Or, just to confuse you, restaurants will use colors like green or red. I personally recommend that you avoid the "blue" variety. The problem is further complicated because after you choose your hot sauce, you are usually required to choose a drink size, and you can only hope that you get one that suits the strength of the hot sauce. Either you end up trying to put out a match with a fire hose, or trying to stop a forest fire with a squirt gun.

Normally I just like to complain about things without proposing a solution, but this time an answer occurred to me after the nurse read me my bedtime story. I'd like to suggest the Goldilocks labeling system, to be implemented by all fast-food restaurants immediately under threat of martial law. All restaurants, from this point forward, shall only have the following drink sizes:

Too Big, Too Small, and Just Right. A similar system will be used for hot sauce.

So there it is. I hope this hasn't been too much for you. If you wanted more, you should have ordered the regular, whatever that is.

Reigning Cats and Dogs

I laughed as I drove down the freeway. A sign posted on the back of the truck in front of me said, "Canine massage therapy." Instantly an entire day spa for dogs sprung to life before my eyes: poodles in mud baths, German shepherds lying on cots with cucumber slices over their eyes, and dachshunds wearing towels around their waists while masseuses gave them rub downs.

It could be that I didn't know exactly what they meant by "canine massage therapy," but I was already off on my own tangent, so that had become irrelevant. I couldn't help but think that my *wife* was lucky if she got an afternoon at the spa, so I found it hard to imagine sending a dog to one. As far as that goes, the dogs I have owned seemed pretty happy—downright ecstatic, actually—when I gave them a chew toy. They acted as if it was manna from heaven, a gift from the gods. I would hardly expect such an excited, jumping-up-and-down, slobbering-all-over-the-floor elation in response to a free coupon to the doggy masseuse. My last dog, Doofus (not his real name), would have eaten the coupon and thanked me for the snack.

Our last pet, Bubba, was a beta fish, and I wonder now if we were neglectful in how we treated him. Should we have taken him to the movies with us? Should we have fed him steak instead of those fishy smelling pellets? Did we fail him because we should have installed a flat screen TV in his tank rather than that ceramic coral he liked to hide under? Should he have had TiVo?

Perhaps the pets I have owned just weren't sophisticated enough. Doofus, for example, liked to dig holes in the backyard. This was his single greatest joy, and he could not, it seemed, be deprived of it. Oh, sure, I tried. I gave him a badminton set, even a Jet Ski. But, besides gnawing on them (and peeing on the Jet Ski), he pretty much ignored these gifts and went on back to digging holes in the yard. I even tried reading books to him. I started with the classics and then, when he paid no attention, I turned to murder mysteries. All I got was a vacant stare and the occasional bark.

The cats I've owned have been even harder to please. They acted so snooty that I wouldn't have been surprised to catch them sitting out on the patio, having wine and caviar—one of them starting up the barbecue with its furry little paws, getting ready to grill some shrimp kebobs. Here again, I tried to get my cats' interest, especially my last cat, Buffy the Lizard Slayer. I showed Buffy pictures of ideal vacation spots, holding her pink kitty nose up to the computer screen. I even bought her ballet slippers. But she reacted with disdain—a total lack of interest.

I think back to when, as a kid, I had a hamster. It used to love to run for hours on the wheel in its cage, but now I'm wondering if a more modern treadmill would have been in order. Or maybe a Bowflex exercise machine. My hamster's abs were always a bit flabby, and she never really did look good in a swimsuit.

In retrospect, I feel so selfish. During that summer I spent in Yermo learning how to ride a horse, and during all that time I spent brushing its hair and cleaning its hooves, never once did it occur to me to take it to Disneyland. What kind of person am I? I have failed as a pet owner and as a human being.

I guess I'll never understand animals, at least, not like some people do. Not like those who take their gerbils to astrologers or those who call in sick to work because their cat has the sniffles (true story). And not like those who use the services of pet psychics to get inside the complicated workings of the minds of their animal friends. All I've ever had to offer was food, companionship, and a healthy dose of affection. So to you guys with the massage therapy business—good luck with that. But if I were you, I'd keep some doggy biscuits in reserve, right next to the hot steamy towels.

Patty Melts

If you want to cause chaos and panic in your local Wienerschnitzel, go through their drive-thru and order a patty melt. Now and then, I do it just for fun. I also do it because I love patty melts. If luck is with me, I'll get one. When I'm not so lucky, I'll get a chocolate shake with a slice of cheese in it.

In the old days, back when there was a "Der" before the "Wienerschnitzel," patty melts used to be on the Der Wienerschnitzel menu right next to all the hotdogs. You could order a patty melt, and they wouldn't even flinch. Then, one day, some manager high up in the Wienerschnitzel corporate office got what he or she thought was a "great idea." In management, as I'm sure some of you are aware, a "great idea" is something that is implemented without any consideration of what kind of consequences it might have, sometimes resulting in catastrophe. This particular great idea was to remove patty melts from the Wienerschnitzel menu and needlessly complicate my life. But I didn't let this stop me. I kept ordering them. After awhile, though, it began to cause confusion. People at the drive-thru didn't know how to ring it up. Sometimes they would ask me how to make it. "One slice of cheese or two?" or "Does that go on rye bread?" I did my part to make the world a better place and patiently explained the answers.

I had this system going well when a Wienerschnitzel marketing weasel had a great idea. "Let's bring the patty melt back as a temporary promotion!" he, she, or it, said. They also added a caveat: "Let's put chili on it." So now I had to order my patty melts with no chili.

Of course, this promotion ended quickly, immediately making things worse for patty melt lovers nationwide (I know you're out there). The next time I ordered a patty melt, the girl at the drive-thru said, "We don't make those anymore."

I tried to explain to her that I used to order patty melts before the patty melt promotion was a blister on some marketing weasel's swollen head. "I ordered patty melts before you started making them again," I said. Despite the clarity of my explanation, she wasn't going for it. She insisted that they could not make patty melts regardless of the fact that they had all the necessary ingredients to do so. I drove away from the restaurant empty-handed and empty-stomached. For some time after that, I ended up going twenty miles farther to another Wienerschnitzel that didn't argue with me about taking my money.

Then they built a Wienerschnitzel even closer to me. Happily, the manager of the store was completely familiar with patty melts. The drive-thru girl told me that he sometimes made them for himself when he was at lunch. In a flash, the order of the universe was properly restored.

It stayed that way for at least a week. The order of the universe is a fickle thing (as opposed to a deluxe dog, which, I believe, is a pickle thing). The new Wienerschnitzel had a problem with employee turnover (as opposed to apple turnovers), and soon I found myself getting patty melts with two patties instead of one, which brings this epic tale to the present day.

I went to Wienerschnitzel this afternoon and ordered a patty melt. I was careful to specify that it should only have one patty. The girl at the drive-thru got that part right, but she kept on referring to the sandwich as a "patty meal." I carefully enunciated it so that she might learn by example, but she failed to catch the hint. When I got to the window, she asked, "Did you want cheese on that patty meal?"

I answered yes, but what I meant to say was, "It's called a patty melt because the *cheese melts* on the hamburger patty! Do you get it now?" That might have overwhelmed her, though, as counting out my change seemed to be taxing enough.

I'll be back there next week. There will be someone new to take my order, and the drama will continue. But do not despair, oh patty melt lovers of America, because I realize that, other than hotdogs, there are few things as American as patty melts, and I intend to keep them alive and well done—one drive-thru at a time.

The Last of Christmas

"That's the last of Christmas," my wife announced, indicating that all the Christmas decorations were put away.

"How about the upholstered wall hanging that's over the fireplace?" I asked.

"Oh," she said, "except for that."

About an hour later I handed her the stuffed reindeer that had been leaning on the stereo.

No doubt, in July I'll be removing a little snowman from a corner hutch, and sometime in mid-September, I'll figure out how to get the glazed Christmas tree off of the patio window.

"The last of Christmas" is a meaningless phrase, kind of like "the end of time." It never arrives.

Some people want Christmas to last all year. They should come live at our house. That's not an offer. I just mean that if they did live at our house, they would know what a year-round Christmas is like. So stop packing.

It is quite possible that I will find the last Christmas decoration approximately a half-hour before Thanksgiving dinner, just before the decorations come out again.

We have six crates of Christmas decorations in our garage. One of them is labeled "Easter," but that's just to throw people off. I'm not sure who, possibly the Christmas detectives, but either way it's misleading.

Now there's a concept—the Christmas detectives. Perhaps we could hire them to snoop around our house and find all the Christmas decorations we haven't put away, like the ornament that somehow ended up in the sock drawer, or the snowflake potholders. I imagine the Christmas detectives would have a dog that sniffs out the Christmas stuff, his nose lighting up like Rudolph's whenever he nears a holiday decoration.

Have you ever played that game Operation? The reason I ask is because the patient in that game has a nose that lights up whenever you fail to correctly remove an item from his body, which makes me wonder if he's related to Rudolph. Frankly, to look at them both, you'd think they'd just had too much eggnog. Maybe that's where the expression "he's lit" came from.

Speaking of lights, I have yet to hang up Christmas lights on the house. If I did, they would never come down, and then we might as well just move to Santa's Village and be done with it. Elves would show up at our door with applications for work. Reindeer would land on the roof and scare away all the pigeons. Snowmen would call us asking for directions, and we'd have to tell them not to come over because we live in Southern California, and they'd melt here!

Maybe I've gotten carried away, but you'll be relieved to know that I've gone just about as far as I can go with this.

I'm done.

I promise.

No more. Not another word.

Except for this one.

And this one.

Sorry.

Christmas! Christmas! Christmas!

Couldn't help it. Again, I apologize. I'm finished now.

Really.

Okay, I'm not, but I could have been.

Now I'm through.

Tell you what, I'll stop typing, and that'll be the last of this whole Christmas thing.

For now.

See what I'm saying? It never ends.

Fine Dining

"So, it's come to this, has it?" I said to my wife.

She stood there with a knife in her hand and a menacing look in her eye.

How did we get to this place? I wondered. I thought about the incidents that led up to this moment:

We were at a restaurant, our mouths watering with the thought of a great Italian meal. The greeter led us to our table. For a second I thought that they had already prepared a meal for us because, when we got to our table, there were enough bread crumbs on the seats to make a full course dinner. Across the table was a big red trail of spaghetti sauce. The greeter thoughtfully dipped our menu into the sauce as if it was an appetizer and then left.

We stared at the table. We looked back at the entrance. My wife went to go get someone to clean up.

The person who came to help us had a scowl on her face and a towel in her hand. She used the towel to smear the spaghetti sauce in a wider swath across the table, and then she placed the menu right back on top of the sauce. If, at that moment, somebody had asked me, "What's on the menu?" I could have answered, "Spaghetti sauce. Oh, and a noodle."

"Excuse me," I called to the girl with the towel, but she had already leapt away like an antelope pursued by a lion.

We stared at the table, and then we turned around and left.

Sadly, this experience was followed by similar experiences at a variety of local restaurants. We no longer expect good customer service, cleanliness, or even the meal we ordered. We hope for them, but we are well aware that the restaurant industry has deemed these things to be optional. It's random. It's a mood thing.

At one restaurant we went to, they brought me the wrong sandwich, then they brought the right sandwich, but with globs of mayonnaise, when I had requested it without. After I cleaned the sandwich off and started eating it, they brought out a third sandwich, also covered in mayo. They tried to serve it to us despite the fact that we were both already eating. We graciously declined. We even laughed as we told our waitress about it.

"That's funny," she said, frowning all the while. Then she promptly brought us the bill, which included charges for twice as many sandwiches as we had ordered.

Then there was the restaurant where, when we went to sit down, there was a big chunk of meat on the seat. Not only did the silverware have unidentified stains on it, but so did our waitress's face. She had to go on break because her pimp was trying to get ahold of her on her cell phone. All right, the last sentence isn't true, but it *could* have been true.

Which brings us back to the present day. I got home from work and my wife was in the one room in our house that we never use. I went in to see what was going on.

"What are you doing?" I asked.

"Cooking."

"Never heard of it. What's that mean?"

"It's this thing that some of the ladies at my work were talking about. They said that, back in the old days before there were restaurants, people used to make their own meals right in their own homes!"

"You're kidding me!" I said, my mouth agape.

"I know. I couldn't believe it either."

"So, it's come to this, has it?" I said.

She stood there with a knife in her hand and a menacing look in her eye. Then she sliced a tomato clean in half. "Yes, it has," she answered. "Yes, it has."

Salami and Cheese

I could easily live on salami and cheese. Stick me in a bunker somewhere with nothing but a refrigerator stocked with those two foods and maybe some crackers and water, and I'd be perfectly happy until the rations ran out.

Knowing this, picture me dragging my feet to another meeting with the Accounting Department to discuss such invigorating topics as sales tax overrides and electronic invoicing. Now imagine my sudden change of attitude as I see that someone has thoughtfully supplied us with a snack for the meeting: salami, cheese, and crackers. My posture went from slouched to erect, my expression from glum to eager, and I took a quick detour to the vending machine for a Pepsi.

I entered the conference room and took a seat nearest to the plate.

"Let's get this meeting started," I announced, fixing myself a cracker and popping open my drink. I had no qualms about being the first one to dig in.

As the meeting continued and we went through the action items from our last meeting, I only had one thought. It was not what the aging for the Collections Department was, nor was it the question of how we could adjust sales orders to allow for the Florida sales tax cap. It was this: *Why isn't anyone else eating the salami and cheese? What is wrong with these people?*

I waited for what I considered to be an acceptable amount of time before I helped myself to seconds. It only made me hungrier. In the distance, I heard someone mumbling about accounts payable. *How long must I wait before I take another bite?* I wondered.

You know what? I rationalized. *Obviously, no one else here is interested in the plate of salami and cheese. So it's only fitting that I eat more. Why should I wait? Everyone else is probably so absorbed in the meeting that they won't even notice what I'm doing.*

I reached toward the food just when a manager from another department did the same. Our hands nearly touched the plate at the same time like with Judas and Jesus at The Last Supper. I quickly withdrew my hand.

I was struck by an odd mixture of emotions. I was grateful that the manager had taken some food because that meant I would look like less of a pig. But I was angry because he had taken what was rightfully MINE. *It's mine, I tell you! Mine! Mine! It's all mine!*

I took a deep breath.

"Bruce, do you have the numbers for the credit memos and returns this month?" somebody asked.

"Huh?" I cleverly responded. "Oh. Sorry. Yes. Yes. I do. Here they are." I flipped through my papers and rapidly read off the figures.

"How many remain from the third quarter again?" the person keeping minutes asked me.

"Cheese," I answered. "I mean three."

She gave me a funny look and then wrote down the number.

Whew. I had contributed my part to the meeting. That only meant one thing: it was time for my reward. I reached for the plate when someone asked me to pass it down. I did. I can only hope that she didn't notice the glare I gave her.

Certainly, I had now earned another serving. I leaned to the side so that I was closer to the food, possibly invading too much of a coworker's space.

"Excuse me," I said, my arms outstretched so that my fingers nearly touched the edge of the plate. Someone from Accounting was kind enough to push it in my direction.

I grabbed another serving and wolfed it down. And then—at this point I could no longer control myself— another, leaving only enough for one more person. I couldn't take that too, could I?

The last ten minutes of the meeting were excruciating. My eyes kept straying back to the plate. How could anyone not notice that the last helping was sitting there like that and not eat it? Seasons passed—spring, summer, the changing leaves of fall—before the meeting came to an end.

No one had claimed the prize. As people got up from their chairs, I pulled the plate closer to me and ate directly from it.

"Hey Bruce," one of the managers from our department said, "I'll need that action item completed by end of business tomorrow."

Action item? I thought. *What action item?* Out loud I said, "Okay! I'll get right on that."

I shoved the rest of the salami into my mouth. *Maybe nobody noticed my slight obsession*, I told myself. *Maybe I had made it too much of a big deal in my own mind.*

"Hungry, Bruce?" one of the collectors asked. She winked, smiled, and turned towards the door. I wiped some crumbs from my mouth and then looked down at the conference room table. It looked like Cookie Monster had been there.

Oops. I blushed even though there was no one left in the conference room but me. I guess that, sometimes, the only person you fool is yourself. I filled the room with a loud burp and then went back to work. If, as a Christmas bonus, I receive a gift certificate for The Swiss Colony, I shouldn't be surprised.

Comedy Traffic School

Drunk driving is not funny, but sometimes the actions of drunk drivers are, especially when the police pull them over before they can cause any damage. Take, for example, the guy who placed a large traffic cone over his head and began twirling around in front of the police officer. Or the guy who fell backwards into the grass while the officer was talking to him. My personal favorite was the guy who, when asked if he spoke English, picked up a traffic cone, held it to his mouth like a megaphone, and shouted, "No!"

These fine gentlemen were all featured in a videotape shown in Comedy Traffic School, which I recently attended because I received my first traffic ticket in over fifteen years. The ticket, if you must know, was for speeding, which is apparently illegal in Norco, California. I told the officer that I had gone over the speed limit in other cities, and *they* never gave me a ticket. The officer then wrote me up for having a broken taillight, and I decided that maybe I should let him do his job.

The videotape excerpts that I mentioned above (you may not be surprised by this) were the only genuinely funny parts of the full eight hours of Comedy Traffic

School. The rest of the jokes were allegedly funny, meaning that they might possibly be funny, but it would be real hard to prove.

At the start of the class, our instructor pretended to be of Middle Eastern descent long enough for us to believe he was for real. The comedy value of this is unclear. When the instructor stopped and began acting like a guy from California who teaches traffic school, we all fidgeted in our seats and became even more uncomfortable than your average traffic school attendees already are. My palms started to sweat.

Perhaps our instructor had not heard comedy rule number 518, which states that irritating people who are already grumpy is not likely to make them laugh. For example, if you have a headache, and I jab you with a sharp stick, you are not likely to say, "Boy, Bruce, you are a comedy laugh riot. Please provide me with more hilarity."

This was the first of many laws of comedy to be violated and, during the day, several citable offenses occurred. For example, one can have his comedy license revoked in certain states (and coincidentally, Norco) for overusing the phrase "You're scaring me" in one's attempts at humor.

Another of the "gags" pulled by our instructor was that he told us that we could make our tires last longer by occasionally deflating them and then filling them back up with air. He said, very officially, that stale air molecules attach themselves to the inside of the tire and wear it down from the inside while all the other forces wear the tire down from the outside. He then revealed that this was a joke.

Comedy rule number eight states that if you have to explain that what you just said was a joke, the odds are that it was not funny. This is why the phrase "just kidding" is a giveaway that a joke has failed. For the sake of clarity, I must mention that written comedy is an exception to this rule because it is an entirely different art form than spoken comedy. Another exception is when you are being deliberately obtuse, as I have been guilty of on occasion, like that time I told my goldfish that its real name was Bernie.

"Was that a joke?" you ask. I'm not telling.

By the end of Comedy Traffic School, I had laughed a few times in a kind of giddy insane way. This is because stale air molecules had attached themselves to the inside of my head, and I was starting to wear down.

Immediately after receiving my certificate of completion from Comedy Traffic School, I slapped down my "Comedy Police" badge and issued the instructor a citation. No doubt, he will try to keep it off his record by going to Comedy Comedy School. Regardless, justice was served. And so was dessert because I had some pie when I got home.

Just kidding. That was a joke.

Coprolite

I don't often indulge in scatological humor, but now and then a guy just has to unload. I wouldn't even mention it if it wasn't related to something scientific in nature, and that just happens to be the case.

I was at a museum with a geologist friend of mine, and I noticed something odd in one of the displays.

"Hey!" I exclaimed. "That looks like a huge—"

"Yes," my geologist friend said. "That is fossilized dinosaur poo."

"You're kidding!" I read the plaque and saw that my friend was not, shall we say, "pooing" me.

"That is awesome!" I added. I could barely contain my excrement—I mean excitement. This was the best thing I had ever seen in a museum. I memorized the name of it, and my geologist buddy helped me on the pronunciation. It is called coprolite.

"I can't believe they have it on display," I commented. "Those scientific types certainly must think a lot of dinosaurs."

I couldn't have been more right. I discovered later, in a book by Carl Sagan called *The Dragons of Eden*, that there were many theories about the extinction of the dinosaurs. On page 145, I read the following about such theories: "All the explanations proposed seem to be only partly satisfactory. They range from massive climatic change to mammalian predation to the extinction of a plant with apparent laxative properties, in which case the dinosaurs died of constipation."[1] Amazing.

But there was more. In *A Short History of Nearly Everything*, Bill Bryson tells about the Reverend William Buckland. Mr. Buckland inspired Charles Lyell's interest in geology, and Charles Lyell's book *The Principles of Geology* would later have a great influence on Charles Darwin's work. But that's all beside the point. The main object of interest is that William Buckland became an authority on coprolite and "had a table made entirely out of his collection of specimens."[2] How cool is that?

My discovery of coprolite prompted many jokes of an anti-intellectual nature that I shall not torment you with, except to say that they eventually turned into <u>a series of tales</u> involving Corporal Coprolite and his

1   Carl Sagan, *The Dragons of Eden* (New York: Ballantine Books, 1986), p. 145.
2   Bill Bryson, *A Short History of Nearly Everything* (New York: Broadway Books, 2003), p. 69.

faithful sidekick, Private Pisalot. I am, after all, a male of the species, and, by default, I am incapable of ever completely growing up. Please don't use this as an excuse to dump on me. It would be a waste.

My geologist friend explained to me that Steven Spielberg wanted to focus more on the coprolite angle in the *Jurassic Park* films. I expressed some doubt, but then my buddy said, "Oh yeah, what do you think *Park* is backwards?"

Stunned by this revelation, I gained a new respect for Steven Spielberg. "That certainly explains the reviews the film got," I said.

"Boy, what else does this museum have?" I continued, hoping to discover something like *The Toilets of the Gods*.

"I'm afraid that's the best of it," my friend answered.

But he was wrong. When we got to the Egyptian exhibit, we learned that the Egyptians thought their intellect resided within their hearts, so when the Egyptians mummified the Pharaohs, they kept the Pharaohs' hearts, but pulled their brains out of their noses and threw them out.

"Maybe that's what happened to you," my buddy said.

"Coprolite Head," I responded.

"Don't think you can make me the butt of your jokes, Pharaoh Brain!"

"Coprolite Head," I answered.

"Pharaoh Brain!" he yelled back.

It was then that security escorted us out.

Anyway, I really enjoyed our trip to the museum. It was very educational. You should go. Then you can become an intellectual, just like me.

Duhsa

When I received my first Mensa membership card in the mail, I said to myself, "Yay! I'm smart!" When I went to put the card away, I realized I had lost my wallet, and I said to myself, "Bruce, you're an idiot." I live with this dichotomy every day. One second I'm brilliant, the next I'm, er, non-smart. I'd venture to say that this applies to other people besides me. Many of us (again, I'm generalizing and speaking about no one in particular) do stupid things at one time or another, especially my friend Roger.

That is why I'm starting up a club called "Duhsa," which is open to everybody.

Duhsa: because everybody does stupid things.

It's pretty easy to get into *Duhsa*; you just have to fail the entrance exam, which is based on the fact that people with all kinds of intelligence (including spatial, mathematical, verbal, and emotional intelligence) seem to have trouble filling out forms correctly. Here is the exam in its entirety:

What is your name?

That's it. You get to take it twice, just so you have a fair chance. I failed both times. The first time I spelled my name wrong. (I spelled it "Brus" just like I had seen the hostess at a restaurant spell it.) The second time, I cheated and copied off the guy next to me. His name, apparently, was a Social Security number.

If you still doubt that I am qualified to be a *Duhsa* member, take the following facts into consideration.

Fact 1) I have been known to get into the driver's side of a car and with my right hand, slam the door on my left hand. Apparently the two sides of my body were not communicating at the time they did this. Since that time, they have flat out refused to talk.

Fact 2) I once wrote a check for the entire balance of my checkbook to the Mobil Oil Corporation. Helpful tip: do not drink wine while doing your finances.

Fact 3) When I was young (and that is my only excuse), I left a car on an uphill incline with the engine running and without putting the car in park. Shortly after I got out of the car, it (surprise!) started rolling down the hill. I chased the car part of the way down the hill, possibly thinking that I could stop it with my bare hands and thereby impress Lana Lang. I failed to do either. At the bottom of the hill, the car swerved and slid into a tree, becoming wedged under a huge tree limb. The ground underneath the car was dirt, so when I got in and tried to drive, I only succeeded in producing a rooster tail of earth and dust.

This happened out in the boonies, long before there were cell phones, so I had to walk two miles to a store, buy an axe, and return to the scene of my stupidity to chop the tree limb off. Fortunately, it worked. Once again, I was free to drive the streets and endanger the lives of others.

I am not only the *Duhsa* president; I am also a member.

I figured that *Duhsa* could have annual gatherings once every four years. We could also hold regional gatherings for everybody in the county. Topics for seminars would include "I watch daytime television even though I know better," "Where are my keys?" and "Speling."

The purpose of *Duhsa*? To figure out why it is that every time I start feeling arrogant, I turn around and do something so idiotic that it undermines any credibility or appearance of intelligence I may have established. Is there some cosmic mechanism set up to keep me eternally humble? *Duhsa* has funded a foundation to study this and other questions. The foundation consists of many highly paid philosophers who sit around and debate these topics without ever reaching any conclusion.

If any of this sounds good to you and you'd like to join *Duhsa*, please mail me some cash. I recommend sending it in a clear plastic sandwich bag so I can see immediately how much money I'm getting. And don't forget to put your name, address, Social Security number, and birth date on the bag, so I can thank you for contributing to our cause.

Crazy Water

I like snorkeling because it is a funny sounding word. Going out into the water and actually using a snorkel is different. For one thing, the second you put a snorkel in your mouth and a diving mask on your face, you get big fat puffy Angelina Jolie lips. Angelina is, apparently, the only person who looks good with her lips.

The second problem with using a snorkel is that water gets in it. I'm told that in order to clear the snorkel, all one needs to do is exhale sharply, causing a blast of white mist to shoot from the snorkel like the spray from a dolphin's blowhole. I have tried this "exhaling sharply" trick and have concluded that if I were Flipper, I would be dead.

Quick quiz: Which word is funnier?

A) Snorkel

B) Blowhole

Learning to snorkel was part of my training when I became a certified scuba diver. Becoming a certified scuba diver enables you to tell the "certified" joke with all your diver friends. It goes like this:

> Diver One: Are you certified?
>
> Diver Two: Yes.
>
> Diver One: Aha ha ha! (Diver One laughs because the implication is that you are certifiably crazy, rather than certified as a diver. Get it?)

When playing the role of Diver Two, I respond to the laughter by saying, "With friends like you, who needs anemones?" I leave these encounters feeling triumphant because in my own little world, in which I make all the rules, one bad pun wins over an insult by twenty points.

I have several memorable scuba diving experiences. One that always comes to mind is the time my diving buddy swam up to me and flapped his arms like he was a chicken.

I held my hands up and tilted my head to the side, which is the universal diving signal for "Why are you flapping your arms like a chicken?"

My friend pointed behind me. I looked, but didn't see anything. Later, when we surfaced, I came face to face with a sea lion.

"That's what I was trying to tell you about," said my friend. "I saw a seal!"

"I thought you were trying to tell me you saw a chicken," I said.

"Why would I tell you I saw a chicken? There aren't any chickens in the ocean."

"Right," I agreed. "That's why I thought it was strange."

The conversation went on from there, but as a result of it, I gave my friend a pen and tablet designed for underwater writing. Unfortunately, his handwriting and drawing skills are poor, so we went from playing Ocean Charades to Ocean Pictionary.

I'm told by an unreliable source that techniques for playing Ocean Pictionary are taught in advanced diving classes. While I never took that particular class, I did take one in which I had the chance to do a deep-sea dive and see sunken boats ninety-five feet down off the coast of Catalina Island. Although, I did have some trouble with my buoyancy compensator (BC) on that trip. The BC is an airbag that divers wear. Depending on the depth, you either fill it with air or release air so that you don't sink to the bottom or float to the top. My BC had a leak in it. So about eighty feet below the surface, I filled it up, and because of the leak, I filled it up some more. Then I found myself shooting towards the surface like a cork shot out of a blowhole (or a snorkel; it's your choice).

My diving partner said he looked around and wondered, "Where did Bruce go?" Then he looked overhead and saw me zipping upwards. He later told me that he wondered what the heck I was doing. I told him I saw a seal.

The descent is the hardest part of the dive. I had to do it all over again, but that's what I get for overcompensating.

The thing I enjoy most about scuba diving is how hungry it makes me and how good food tastes afterwards. My theory is that this is why whales are so big. They swim all day, and then, at night, they order huge pizzas with lots of anchovies. They also play Ocean Pictionary. Why doesn't Christian Riese Lassen ever paint that? I envision a scene similar to the infamous poker-playing dogs, and I would love to see it on black velvet.

These days I don't dive much, but occasionally I do throw on my mask, snorkel, and fins and walk around the house—the fins "thwip, thwip, thwipping" against the carpet. Sometimes our guests look at me funny. I don't see what the problem is. I'm certified. But hey, you knew that already.

The Aquarium of the Pacific

Two giant sharks were aimed straight at us, their mouths wide open.

"Hide the Starbursts," I said to my wife, even though the sharks were plastic.

Beyond the sharks were life-size replicas of a blue whale and its newborn calf, hanging from the ceiling on sturdy wires. To the left of us were fish and sea mammals of all shapes and sizes. Some were stuffed animals; some were made of rubber. One of them wore a T-shirt that said, "Aquarium of the Pacific." The ads for the aquarium had been right; there *were* all kinds of sea creatures there.

We had tickets for a 3D movie about the ocean, so we went to see that first. In the movie we discovered another variety of marine life, the computer animated type (subspecies: computergraphicus). They were pseudo-fish, kind of like what you get at Long John Silvers. By the time we left the theater, I was hungry (not literally) for some real fish. Fortunately, the Aquarium of the Pacific had plenty. There were purple fish, blue fish, one fish, two fish. There were fish that matched every color of the rainbow of Starbursts that my wife had in her purse.

Sharron had bought the Starbursts at Vons that morning and had been feeding them to me intermittently. I found myself in some sort of behaviorist experiment where my actions were dictated by positive reinforcement. I don't know why I never thought to take the whole bag from her and just run.

We are the only animals, the 3D film had told us, that have the capacity to implement significant change in our world. *Maybe you are*, I thought.

One of the most interesting exhibits at the Aquarium of the Pacific is, oddly enough, the display of jellyfish. Jellyfish are not to be confused, the sign said, with peanut butter fish, which are an endangered species (of the genus weeatemchunky). In the wild, it is never a good idea to disguise yourself as something that tastes good. This is why there aren't any insects that look like pears (source: Encyclopedia Britannica).

Also at the aquarium was a lorikeet exhibit, which is kind of weird because lorikeets are birds. Apparently somebody at the aquarium got confused about what the word "aquarium" actually means, and they ordered some birds by mistake. They don't even pretend to be embarrassed about it, but frankly, I think it's a big screw up.

Halfway through the day, we left the aquarium to have lunch across the street at the Bubba Gump Shrimp Company. I couldn't bear to eat any fish, having seen so many cute ones swimming around and after learning about all the vicious predators they have to face, so instead I had a lorikeet sandwich.

Okay! I had a cheeseburger. Jeez.

Our ticket to the aquarium also included a boat tour of the Long Beach Harbor. After lunch, we went on the tour and got an opportunity to learn about local marine life (and about some of the guys in the Navy as well). As we sat on the bow of the boat, my wife pointed out a woman who had a sour expression on her face (subspecies: alwayspissedoffidus). We had seen her at different places throughout the aquarium.

"She hasn't cracked a smile all day," my wife observed.

"You know what she needs?" I asked.

"What?"

"Starbursts."

Sharron nodded and fed me one.

I wagged my tail.

Back at the aquarium, we finished looking at the exhibits. In one, there was a huge, round, glass tank where sardines swam in a circle, looking like a perpetual cyclone of tin foil. A young girl in front of us asked her father why the fish just swam around in circles.

"Probably for the same reason I do," he said.

Oddly, after we left the aquarium, that was the main image I carried with me. Monday morning, as I rounded a curve on the freeway interchange, I pictured the fish going around in circles. I wondered if our species really has the ability to change the world, or if we've been conditioned by so many factors that, like our cousins in the sea, we are just swimming, swimming, swimming.

The Grand Canyon

It's a thankless job being the Colorado River. It works very hard with no pay and very little recognition.

"I'll see to it that you get a raise," I said to the river. I doubt that it heard me. I was thousands of feet above it in a helicopter. Otherwise, it probably would have heard me just fine and gurgled a watery "thanks."

Our first view of the Grand Canyon was from the helicopter. The helicopter took us over the desert flatlands of Arizona to the edge of the canyon where it seems as if the world drops away. The canyon is a jagged landscape of geological puzzle pieces, destined never to be put together. I imagined a zipper big enough to stretch the length of the canyon. If zipped shut, the canyon would draw together, the sides of it crunching into place, and the flat surface of Arizona would be restored to its once pristine shape. Then an announcer would say something about Levi's, a marketing agent would get paid, and hopefully, the Colorado River would get a commission.

This goes to show you that the Grand Canyon, in all its glory, has many different effects on those who view it and that people come away with varied impressions.

Standing on the South Rim, with the Grand Canyon underfoot, I was reminded of a scene in the IMAX film about the canyon, depicting the arrival of the first Spanish explorers. They were walking through the desert, not expecting anything, when suddenly they came upon this vast and colorful chasm.

"Holy cow," they must have said. "We're going to have to go around."

It was interesting listening to the comments of the canyon's modern day visitors. People from everywhere come to see it, from places as far away as Australia, Africa, and Redondo Beach.

"Dude, this is *bleeping* hardcore!" said one such visitor.

One lady sat on a rock at the edge of the canyon smoking a cigarette, and, in a cockney accent, she discussed the virtues of different beauty parlors with her mother.

Parents, visibly excited by the canyon, pointed out features to their children, some of whom clearly seemed bored. "After this," I heard one of them ask, "can we go to the hotel? I want to take a long bath and a nap."

Children often see the wonder in the little things that we take for granted, but sometimes it takes someone who has seen a lot to realize just how impressive the Grand Canyon is. The adults we saw were more thrilled by it than the children.

One lady, after taking our picture for us, said, "Isn't it amazing what God has created?"

Wow, I thought. *She must go to that church where they worship erosion.*

My own impression of the canyon was that it was so massive that it didn't seem real. It made me think of the Grand Canyon diorama on the Disneyland train ride. The rocks could have been made from cardboard, and the view, spanning a thousand miles, could have been painted on canvas and propped up in the back. Standing there, it occurred to me that the Disneyland version of the Grand Canyon was more realistic than I thought, and the Grand Canyon, itself, looked kind of fake. But in those moments when I could convince myself that it was real, it was stunning.

One master of ennui' described the Grand Canyon as "just a really big hole." But it is more than that. It is a really, really big hole.

In the visitor's center, there are a series of pictures of the canyon taken from the same exact spot during different times of day. Each scene looks remarkably different. As the sun makes its way over the canyon, the scene below changes dramatically. The artist Monet was so obsessed with light and its effect upon what we see that he spent hours painting the same haystacks over and over again as the light changed. He would have gone berserk at the Grand Canyon. I found myself similarly obsessed, taking pictures as the colors and shadows of the canyon shifted.

"The light! It's changing again!" I would say to my wife. "Honey? Wait up, Honey!"

Along the southern rim of the Grand Canyon are several structures built by architect Mary Elizabeth Jane Coulter and commissioned by Fred Harvey, who is famous for the Harvey hotels and restaurants that could, prior to World War II, be found at major railway stops. They were like anti-McDonalds, with quality food and quality service. Since then, that sort of thing has gone out of fashion. The history of the South Rim is, of course, even more fascinating now that I have been there, and my exploits—especially the part about where I lost my lens cap—will go down in history.

The structures that Mary Jane Coulter built include the Bright Angel Lodge where we had lunch, the Desert View Watch Tower where we watched the sun set, and the Hopi House where my wife said, "I Hopi we can find some postcards here."

One of the interesting features of the Bright Angel Lodge is the fireplace that is constructed from different layers of rock. Each layer is taken from the different geological layers of the canyon. The entire room was metamorphosed by the fireplace. It made me feel very sedimental. The design was igneous. It's not one of those things that could be taken for granite. I'm sorry.

I apologize for all the geology puns. It's just that the fireplace really rocked.

Other structures built by Mary Coulter are the Lookout Studio and Hermit's Rest. Hermit's Rest is only accessible via the park shuttle or by hiking. We decided not to hike because temperatures were in the 110s. Park personnel had canceled the mule rides because they didn't want the mules to melt.

Using the park's transportation system enabled us to learn about another group of interesting, but rarely talked about, inhabitants of the South Rim—the park's shuttle drivers. These drivers have various temperaments. One was a gentleman who had read books about the canyon and filled us in on facts that we would have otherwise not known or cared about. Another driver was young and very insistent that everyone be safe. If the tourists failed to be safe and tripped on the steps of the bus, the driver would slam the doors on them and run over their feet. We probably would not have learned anything about the third driver expect for the fact that we sat up front next to the nosiest lady this side of the Rio Grande.

She asked the driver every question in the book. "What's your name? Have you been driving this bus for a long time? Do you like driving the bus? How big is the bus? What's the make and model of the bus? Are you married? Do you have children? Do they do drugs? What's the next stop? What time is it? Have you ever been to Florida? Do you have any unusual tattoos? What's the capital of Paraguay? Do you like my shoes? Where does this bus go? Am I bothering you? It sure is hot. Do you think it's hot? How hot does it get here? How cold does it get? Is that Fahrenheit or Celsius? Do you know where I can buy a soda? Have you had any amazing adventures on this bus?"

The lady's husband was an elderly balding man who had clearly lost his mind. He sat there with a goofy grin on his face and would chuckle at odd moments. His wife continued to badger the driver who, surprisingly, answered many of her questions. It was because of this that we gained some interesting insights into the life of a Grand Canyon shuttle driver.

For instance, one time a guy tried to jump out of the window of the bus, and when he hurt his ribs doing so, he sued the Grand Canyon National Park. In another incident, several guys became upset because they were harassed by a younger bus driver who had slammed a door in their faces and ran over their feet. The angry men chose to take it out on *our* bus driver and threatened to commandeer his bus. Our driver told the question lady about how he bravely tricked and outmaneuvered them. The angry men responded by strapping a bomb to the underside of the bus and rigging it so that if the bus ever went under fifty miles an hour, it would explode. The driver performed many heroic acts and eventually diffused the bomb. The driver's story sounded oddly familiar, but I couldn't place where I had heard it before. The Grand Canyon really does have an interesting history.

We spent two days at the South Rim of the Grand Canyon, which was just about right. I had always thought that the Grand Canyon was one of those places that once you saw it, you wouldn't really have any desire to go back. I found that wasn't true. I'd like to go back at Christmas and take pictures of the canyon in the snow. I'd also like to fill the canyon with those colorful little balls from the playground at McDonalds and jump right into the middle of it. I know that sounds crazy, but the Grand Canyon *is* a marvelous wonder of nature, and I left it feeling inspired.

Profundity

I have recently come to the conclusion that life is *inherently* meaningless, although we, as individuals, can assign our own meaning or purpose to it. This is a conclusion that many will disagree with. For example, the Pope called me up the other day and told me I was an idiot.

Not long after that, I received a call from a rabbi, who wanted to know if I was serious about my philosophy or if it was just part of my shtick. "Silly rabbi," I said, "shticks are for kids."

Now I could, if I chose to, use my conclusion that there is no higher purpose for our lives as an excuse to wallow about in existential angst. Fortunately, my philosophy has an addendum that simply states, "If life is a joke, then why not laugh?"

The great thing about the absurdity of life is that many of the ridiculous things we say and do become profound, simply because they reflect the true nature of the universe. Thus, much of what I have said throughout my life goes from being inane to being deeply significant.

The sentences "I fell into a cup of noodles," "My cousin is an argyle sock," or even "Mookity, mook, mooky, mook," all of which I have been known to say, for no reason at all, now have an added meaning. The unprovoked chicken noises I make are no longer considered to be the acts of a crazy man, but are, instead, clues to guide the uninitiated down the paths of understanding.

Excuse me for a second. My phone is ringing.

Sorry. It was the Pope. I wish he would just leave me alone.

Anyway, it is because of my philosophy that I practice "random acts of randomness"—acts that are neither detrimental nor especially helpful to my fellow human beings. Although such acts could enlighten them, should they be receptive to the profundity behind all that is bizarre, strange, and off-the-wall.

Some random acts you can do:

- Apologize for something you never did.

- Pick a word (randomly) out of the dictionary. Insert it in as many conversations as you can. The word "persnickety" is a good one.

- Buy a stuffed animal. Name it. Have conversations with it. Make it talk to other people.

- Dig something out of the trash and frame it. Give it to someone you barely know.

The next day, ask for it back.

Not only is performing random acts fun, but it has additional side benefits. It enables you to become receptive to new ideas and tolerant of concepts that you previously regarded as strange. Plus, if enough people perform random acts of randomness, it widens the range of what society considers to be acceptable behavior, thereby enabling me to get away with being just a little bit weirder.

And that's really what it's all about; isn't it?

Problems with This Column

Recently, I have received several complaints about this column, and I would like to take this time to lay those problems to rest. The first complaint comes from a bunch of hypocritical complainers who complain that I spend far too much time complaining. My column is always about unhappy things, they claim, such as bad customer service, my sinuses, and people being eaten alive by kitchen appliances.

I tried to explain to my critics that that's the joy of writing a humor column—it allows you to look forward to bad things happening so that you can blow them out of proportion and turn them into hilariously demented romps of self-pity.

"But, you can be happy and funny at the same time," they told me. "Try telling more puns. Everybody loves a good pun!"

As a result of this, I am changing the format of the column, and this column you are reading right now is the first in a series of one, on the theme of "Things Gone Right." This is especially convenient because, this month, not one single bad thing happened to me. In fact, every moment of every day was perfect. Except, that is, for the complaints about this column, which ruined everything.

I would also like to demonstrate that I am not an unhappy person by expressing the one thing that I am thankful for. I do this every Thanksgiving—*every single* Thanksgiving—when I say, "I am thankful that I have hands instead of flippers." And I truly am.

The second complaint I received is that this column isn't weird enough. When I first started *Fun with Stuff*, my intent was to be unflinchingly, unapologetically, and unabashedly bizarre. Sadly, I have failed in this.

Far too often, my column has been relatively normal. Occasionally, entire columns have focused on a single topic and have not jumped from random thought to obscure observation like I had originally planned. The column ceased to be the ramblings of a crazed madman and became the ramblings of a sober madman. For this, I apologize, and it will stop immediately.

I even titled the column *Fun with Stuff* so that I would be at liberty to write about whatever I darn well please, which is why none of us really knows what the next column is going to be like (except for Jane Slickmore, the column psychic, of whom I'm sure you've all heard).

By the way, Jane predicts that my next column is going to be something that very precisely coincides with the column title. It will be both fun and about stuff. (That Jane; she's amazing. I wonder how she does it.)

In case you do not believe me when I tell you that people have requested that I be bizarre, here are some items that actual readers have suggested I include in columns:

> Dogs eating plastic coat hangers
>
> Frogs with machine guns
>
> A chicken that latches onto you and sucks blood

I swear to you. This is the truth.

One discussion about *Fun with Stuff* grew deeply philosophical and resulted in a review of the following questions:

> If a tree falls in the forest and there is no one there to hear it, does it make a noise?
>
> Does a bear (you know what) in the woods?

We concluded that if a bear was in the woods and a tree fell on him, he would probably do his business right there. Undoubtedly, he would be full of sound and furry.

There's your pun. Are you happy now?

So now you know what I'm up against and what to look forward to in future columns. Next month's topic is "Nothing Bad Happened" and will consist entirely of puns based upon unimaginable circumstances. I'm sure you're looking forward to it as much as I am.

Editor's note: the above column is in violation of The Bad Joke Regulation Authority guidelines. It was our intention to have it removed from the publication, but we were unable to catch it in time. We apologize for any inconvenience this may have caused.

Music

Sharron and I were at a convention in Long Beach, California, sharing an elevator with three other people: a lady and two guys. One of the guys, with no apparent provocation, started singing "Oh Danny Boy." The lady, who was standing between him and us, promptly put her finger to her nostril and accompanied him by humming through her nose. The third guy joined in. I have been to many concerts, but none of them stick in my mind quite like that one performance. And it is in the spirit of that performance that I thought I'd share nine musical facts.

Fact 1) When she was young, my sister's name was Mary Smith. She refused to check into hotels under her real name. Fortunately, when she got older, she married a man by the name of Jack Christmas and everything was okay. When she got pregnant with her first child, she got an ultrasound and found out that it was going to be a boy. I asked her what she was going to name him, and she told me she was going to name him Dwight.

"Why did you choose that name?" I asked.

"Well," she said, "I used to know a guy named Dwight who was kind and gentle and a wonderful human being. I want my son to grow up to be just like him."

"Oh, I see," I replied. "You're dreaming of a Dwight Christmas, just like the one you knew before."

Fact 2) In the movie *The Sound of Music,* the Von Trapp family flees Austria to escape the Nazi regime. Later on in history, many of the Nazi war criminals had to flee Austria to South American countries to escape prosecution. This was the inspiration for the song "Don't Crime for Me Argentina."

Fact 3) I believe that when I open up the refrigerator to put a six-pack of Budweiser inside, the beer hears the sound of the refrigerator opening up, and it makes the beer happy. I like to think that it's music to my beers.

Fact 4) The last few things I made up, but this one, I guarantee you, is a "true" fact. On one of the albums by the rock group Kansas, there is a song about a man who is living a dangerous life in apocalyptic times. It's called "Grand Fun Alley." Get it! Grand Finale! Those wacky Kansas guys have been coming up with clever titles ever since that "Ducks in the Wind" song.

Fact 5) LeAnn Rhymes. My question is, with what?

Fact 6) Long before there were compact discs, there were these round things called "records." They were usually made of black vinyl, but for a while, there was a marketing gimmick in which the records were released in different colors. As a result, I have a copy of *Hotel California* in green vinyl. In response to this trend, record companies began releasing records with pictures on them. That was their vinyl answer.

Fact 7) Recently, a lot of classic rock bands have been touring the country. In one case, the Who and the Guess Who were performing together at a nearby stadium. I wanted to know what order the bands were playing in so I asked a friend, "Who's on first?"

Him: That's right.

Me: No, I'm asking you, who's on first?

Him: Yes.

Me: Let me put it this way: who's on second?

Him: Guess Who.

Me: No, you tell me.

Him: I did. Guess Who.

Me: Forget it. Let's talk about baseball.

Fact 8) Two other classic bands, The Rolling Stones and Styx, were playing at the local stadium. A friend of mine lives near the stadium, and he reported that concertgoers totally trampled his lawn, breaking many of his garden gnomes. He said that when female musicians like Pat Benatar were in concert, he never had trouble with people ruining his lawn. "Styx and Stones," he explained, "may break my gnomes, but dames will never hurt me." That's what he said.

Fact 9) I am out of musical facts. Have a nice day.

The Joke Workshop

Most of this story is true. The names have been changed to protect the innocent.

Recently, I went to a conference where I attended a joke workshop. The workshop was led by a lady who has worked with many standup comedians over the years and has written for television sitcoms. The first thing I noticed upon entering the workshop was that the lady was abrasive. I had expected (maybe this was an unfair preconception) that somebody leading a workshop on how to write jokes would be funny. This lady, let's call her Punchy, kept harassing the audience about moving to the front of the room. When we entered, she nearly took me by the hand and led me to the second row. I hate being in front, but I obliged because she was pretty forceful about it.

Punchy gave us handouts listing a series of jokes and asked us to read them. Various members of the audience stood up and read the jokes, while Punchy provided commentary. If someone complained that they could not hear, Punchy was very precise about pointing out that if everyone had come to the front of the room like she had told them to, then, "EVERYBODY COULD

HEAR THE JOKES!" Nobody complained about that anymore.

As the workshop progressed, it became evident that many people had come directly from the "How to be Stubborn and Not Follow Directions" workshop and had successfully mastered those techniques.

The task was simple. Read jokes from the handouts. But people kept trying to tell their own jokes.

There was a baldheaded man who started to tell a joke about a lady who was trying to get on a bus, but Punchy said, "Please only read the jokes that are on the sheet that I passed out."

"How about this one," he said, and he began to read a joke that he had just written, although we had not yet gotten to the point in the workshop where we were supposed to be writing jokes. Punchy stopped him again and made him sit down.

Several people came into the workshop and sat down in the middle of the auditorium.

"Sit near the front," ordered Punchy.

Audience members turned around and gave the newcomers a look that said, "Maybe you should do what she says." The newcomers moved up a couple rows.

The seminar went smoothly for several minutes. As people read the jokes from the handouts like they were supposed to, Punchy pointed out that each of the jokes started out with something that was true from the comedian's point of view. After the initial statement of truth, the comedian was free to go berserk and make whatever twist on the original concept that he or she felt like making. These jokes exemplified the process we were going to use to write jokes in this workshop. We would follow three steps. Step one was to write down something that we loved or hated. It had to be true from our individual perspective. Step two was to give details about it. Step three was to make it funny by exaggerating it, by turning it around, or by whatever method we chose.

At each step, Punchy called on volunteers to read what they had so far. I found it interesting that sometimes all it took to get people to laugh was a simple statement of truth. This had already been demonstrated by some of the jokes we read earlier. Please jot this note down in your list of comedy tips: Sometimes things are funny just because they are true.

Among the jokes that people read, there were some that had promising starts. Of course, a few "instructionally challenged" members of the audience had gone on to steps two and three of our assignment. Punchy had to stop them. The baldheaded guy again started to tell his favorite joke about the lady getting on the bus, but Punchy cut him off. I was starting to see why she was the way she was.

Great. On to Step two: add details to your true statement. So far my joke read as follows. True statement:

I hate the dryers in my apartment complex. More detail: You put your clothes in them for an hour and they still come out wet.

I was following the instructions.

The instructor took this opportunity to point out to the class that the auditorium was filling up, so it would be a good idea if we all moved toward the front of the room so latecomers would have a place to sit.

Punchy went around the room and asked people to read what they had so far. Several people did well. Several other people told jokes they remembered from their childhood. One lady read a joke from the sheet that Punchy had passed out at the beginning of the class. Overall, it was a smashing success.

Now for the fun part. We would get to finish our joke. This would be the most freeform part of the three steps—perfect, you would think, for those who are deaf to guidelines and like to do as they choose. Make your joke funny; that's all we had to do.

I took my story about the dryers and added a little twist to it. The full joke went like this: I hate the dryers in my apartment complex. You put your clothes in them for an hour and they still come out wet. I went to complain to the management, and they asked me how many quarters I used. "Quarters?" I replied.

Cute, but it worked, and it followed the format. I wrote a second one that my wife totally hates, but I can't resist telling it here.

Truth: I hate mayonnaise.

Detail: Because it looks like pus.

Comedy ending: I went to a restaurant and they asked me if I wanted mayo on my sandwich. I said, "Yes and could I have some scabs on that too?"

It still makes me laugh. My wife still hates it.

Punchy had members of the class read their completed jokes. She specified that we should not read jokes about bodily functions or bodily fluids, which ruled out my last joke, as brilliant as it is. We were also not to tell jokes that were off-color or racist in nature.

A lady behind us stood up and told a joke that I don't recall. The next person told one about a "Chinaman." The baldheaded guy told his joke about the lady who was getting on the bus. Punchy was too emotionally drained to stop him. The joke went like this:

> A lady is getting on a bus, and she falls down. She gets up and tries to board the bus again but hits her leg on the first step and tumbles back to the pavement. She gets up again, hits her head on the bus's rearview mirror, and lands in the gutter.

The bus driver says, "Lady, you don't need a bus. You need an ambulance."

The class of about 150 people just stared at the bald guy.

He sat down.

The lady behind us stood up again.

"Ma'am," Punchy said, "you've already read us one of your jokes. Why don't you have a seat, and we'll let somebody else who hasn't had a chance read theirs."

"But it's a really good joke," said the lady.

"I'm going to give some other people a chance first," Punchy said, and she called on somebody else. The lady behind us did not sit down until the other person started reading their joke.

Punchy went around the room, and several of the jokes were pretty good. When nobody laughed at a joke, Punchy, in her own unique style, told the person why the joke wasn't funny, thereby leaving the person emotionally scarred and afraid to ever tell a joke again in his or her life.

The lady behind us stood up again.

"All right," said Punchy, "I've been around the room once; you can read your joke now."

"Well," the lady prefaced, "it's a little bit off-color, so I'm not sure if I should read it."

"If it's off-color, then you're right. You shouldn't read it."

"No, I'm sure it will be okay," the lady answered, then she read her joke. The only thing I remember about it was that it was completely inappropriate.

Just then, a large noisy group of people came into the conference room and sat in the very back row when there were still several open rows in front of them.

Punchy pulled out a machine gun and shot us all dead.

That's my joke.

Something to Write About

I have a lot to write about, but what if I didn't? It occurred to me that I could very easily write about the fact that I had nothing to write about, which would be very similar to this, even though, in this case, I have other things to write about but have chosen not to write about them.

You might be thinking that I don't really have anything to write about and that I'm just saying that I do to make you think that I do. I considered writing a list of topics that I could have written about in order to prove that I did have something else to write about, but that would be silly. I don't really feel the need to justify that I have something else to write about. Surely, someone who can write this much about "what to write about" could come up with something else to write about. Creatively, there are all sorts of options, but for my purposes here, it is best not to stray too far from the main topic and to keep my focus, which is, very simply, to write about "what to write about" without ever writing about anything else. *That* is what I'm writing about.

Now that I've clarified what I'm writing about, which as you read previously, is "what to write about," and now that I've specified that I should not digress too far from that topic, I am not left with too many options. Presenting a list of "things I have now prevented myself from writing about" would be as pointless as providing a list of things I could have written about, if not more so. Even though the whole point of this little escapade is to be relatively pointless, I am attempting to be pointless within certain self-imposed guidelines, which, by their very nature, exclude the actual listing of lists, even though the mentioning of said lists is acceptable. Also be advised that I am not looking for subjects to write about (because I genuinely do have many), and I am aware that the reader may wish that I had chosen any of those other subjects to write about rather than this particular one. If the reader does provide the author with a list of alternate topics, in hopes that I never, ever, chose a topic like this one again, be aware that such lists, along with my own lists, will not be included in this column, not only because of my decision to exclude them, but also because it will be too late. The damage is already done.

I, at this time, would like to thank you for persevering clear through to the end of this column, unless you cheated and skipped ahead to the end, in which case I suggest that you now go back and read the rest because there is a chance (slim, but still a chance) that I hid something interesting in the midst of this column about something to write about. Thank you for joining me.

The Real Me

People have figured it out. I'm not really all that funny. In person, that is. Case in point: I just got back from vacation and people did not walk up to me and say, "Hey Bruce, tell me about your vacation. I'm sure it will be hilarious." Instead, each and every one of them said, "I can't wait to read about your vacation because I'm sure that if you try to tell me about it, I will fall asleep due to your dull and dry verbal delivery."

I don't deny it. Sometimes it's hard to know that I'm even telling a joke.

"Why did Bruce just say that there's an elephant in the refrigerator?" someone will ask.

"Maybe it was a joke," another person will respond.

"But he's not even smiling! Maybe he really thinks there's an elephant in the refrigerator."

"Could be. Personally, I think he's just a fruitcake."

That's why I write humor, so people can add their own tonal inflections to my monotone words. In actuality, it's my readers that are funny, not me. You guys are great! You crack yourselves up.

That might be going overboard. But my point is that if you've never met me, and you expect that I will be as clever in person as I am on paper (however clever you think that is), then you're in for a disappointment. Humor columns are like personal ads. On paper I'm muscular, have sparkling blue eyes, and am six-foot tall. In person I have muscles I haven't used for a long time, my eyes are hidden by my droopy eyelids, and I'm standing on a stool.

Sharron insists that I add a disclaimer saying that I am still very cute because she hates it when I use self-deprecating humor. Frankly, I don't think I'm good enough for self-deprecating humor.

I may not be a comedy laugh riot in person, but if you set me in front of a word processor for a few hours, I will come up with a joke. After several more hours, I will write another one. Over a decade, with multiple rewrites, I can pretend to be glib and quick-witted.

Sharron will see me sitting at the computer scowling at the screen and will ask, "What are you doing? Are you mad about something?"

"I'm writing humor, damnit!" I'll say.

"You better not be making fun of yourself!" she'll answer.

I'll mumble something like, "Dang it, she caught me again," and I'll have to delete everything I wrote. So, you never read this, okay? I'm always funny, all the time. My wife said so.

See, I think Sharron is still a bit confused by our first couple of dates. Normally, I'm pretty quiet, but when I met her I said to myself, *I am going to have to be outgoing and funny if I want to get to know this amazing person I just met.* I was, for a while.

Now and then she'll say to me, "You know, you've been kind of quiet since 1997."

I'll make up some excuse like, "Yeah, I've had a headache." Sooner or later she's going to catch on, and then she'll be like the rest of you.

"Bruce," she'll say, "instead of going to dinner with me, can you just write about what it would be like to go to dinner with me?"

"Sure honey," I'll respond because then I'll know she loves me for who I really am—a billionaire athlete who travels the world in his own private yacht.

Other Books by Bruce A. Smith

How to Get Out of Tough Situations by Being Vague

Women Who Love Women Who Love Men Who Hate Women

The Inner Game of Wickets

The Cow Pie That Ate Rialto

How to Win Friends in Games of Chance

You Can Negotiate Everything if You Want to Annoy Everyone

The Passive Aggressive Handbook

The Bloodsuckers—a gothic horror novel about lawyers (The rights to this book are still being held up in court.)

Fun with Asphalt

Fun with Empty Paper Sacks

Fun with Purple

Chicken Lips Apocalypse

My Pet Peeves (This three-volume collection comes in fine quality handcrafted English leather.)

Todd the Rat

Todd the Rat Goes Fishing

Todd the Rat Goes on Holiday

Love, Look at the Eight of Us

Stuff for Your Truck

The Grapes of Rats